SONGBUILDER

SONGBUILDER

The Life and Music of Guy Clark

Nick Evans & Jeff Horne

First published in 1998 by Amber Waves

Amber Waves is an imprint of Heartland Publishing Limited,
Kingsdown, Warmlake Road, Chart Sutton,
Maidstone, Kent ME17 3RP

ISBN 1 902684 00 1

British Library Cataloguing-In-Publication data

A catalogue record for this book is available from the British Library.

Typeset in Apollo 11pt by the publisher.

Printed and bound in Great Britain by Biddles Ltd., Guildford.

Front cover photograph by Toni Marteney
Back cover photograph from the Travis Clark collection

To the memory of our fathers
Bert and Tommy

Every effort has been made to locate, identify and properly credit photographers. In cases where the photographer is not known, the source or collection which supplied the photograph is stated. Any inadvertent omissions or errors will be corrected in future editions.

Acknowledgment is hereby made for permission to quote song material from the following publishers and copyright holders, to whom all rights are reserved:

Warner Chappell Music, London, for

LA Freeway. Guy Clark ©1972
Desperados Waiting For a Train. Guy Clark ©1973
She Ain't Goin' Nowhere. Guy Clark ©1975
Rita Ballou. Guy Clark ©1975
Let Him Roll. Guy Clark ©1975
Texas–1947. Guy Clark ©1975
Good To Love You Lady. Guy Clark ©1976
Anyhow I Love You. Guy Clark ©1976
Fools For Each Other. Guy Clark ©1978
South Coast of Texas. Guy Clark ©1980

International Music Publishers, London, for

Better Days. Guy Clark ©1983
The Carpenter. Guy Clark ©1983
Immigrant Eyes. Guy Clark & Roger Murrah ©1989
Come From The Heart. Susanna Clark & Richard Leigh ©1989
Boats To Build. Guy Clark & Verlon Thompson ©1992
Ramblin' Jack and Mahan. Guy Clark & Richard Leigh ©1992
Too Much. Guy Clark & Lee Roy Parnell ©1992
Dublin Blues. Guy Clark ©1995
The Cape. Guy Clark, Susanna Clark & Jim Janosky ©1995
Black Diamond Strings. Guy Clark ©1995
Tryin' To Try. Guy Clark & Jimmie Fadden ©1995

CONTENTS

Foreword by Lyle Lovett

A writer like Guy Clark himself is one of the reasons there are other great songwriters.

For me, his writing was a real example to follow, the narrative and the detail in which he writes is so rich. Listening to Guy's songs taught me that it was okay to write about the specific – things that you know about – and have it apply universally. When he tells you about Monahans in *Texas–1947*, that could be a similar experience anywhere in the world. You can write to the small picture and it becomes the big picture. That's how I learned about songs, just listening to songwriters like Guy.

It's so remarkable even to get to meet someone you greatly admire, but to have the privilege of getting to know that person, and then even to work with him, is something else. Guy has been such a friend to me and an influence on me through his music and as a person.

Lyle Lovett, August 1998

INTRODUCTION

IN the summer of 1997 Nick and I were looking for our next publishing project. As musicians, we had been playing the songs of writers like Guy Clark, John Prine and Robert Earl Keen together for years in various lineups, and we happened to pick up two books which triggered off an idea.

The first book, which I had owned for many moons, was *Written in My Soul*, a series of chapter-length interviews with writers, mainly in rock music but also including semi-outsiders like Prine; and the second was Tom Russell and Sylvia Tyson's *And Then I Wrote*, filled with one-paragraph quotes from dozens of primarily roots music songwriters. Finding very little in either book by or about Guy Clark, and, after extensive searching, little more in any printed media, a light bulb went off and the *Come From the Heart* series of books on unsung North American songwriters was conceived.

Gestation was traumatic, but some nine months later we headed across the Atlantic for a fortnight of fascinating interviews and conversations which would form the basis of the first two books we were to write, on Guy Clark and on the Canadian sisters Kate and Anna McGarrigle.

But why Guy Clark anyway?

Well…

In the early 1970s the music you could hear on British radio was at a pretty low ebb. The energy of the progressive rock revolution of the mid to late sixties had dissipated, leaving a sorry collection of outdated musical forms, with little to commend any of it.

But then we started hearing something new. Here were people writing songs which did not fall into any pre-defined category. Apart from feeling vaguely folky/country/bluesy/rocky, there was no convenient pigeonhole they fitted. And but for the presence of people like Charlie Gillett on Radio London, there was no way they would have been heard by a mass audience whose taste was governed and pandered to by pop radio programmers.

This was 'roots music' twenty years before anyone used the term. Gillett's Sunday lunchtime *Honky Tonk* programme was the oasis in a desert of mediocrity that attracted an audience so starved of honest music that its effect was like that of Alan Freed bringing rock'n'roll to American teenagers for the first time.

LA Freeway was the first Guy Clark song I heard on *Honky Tonk*. Jerry Jeff Walker sang it on his eponymous 1972 album, and the sound of its opening lines stopped me with a forkful of shepherd's pie halfway to my mouth:

Pack up all your dishes,
Make note of all good wishes
Say goodbye to the landlord for me –
That sonofabitch has always bored me...

The food went untasted through the four minutes Jerry Jeff, with a typical Clark mixture of weariness and optimism, went through the sweet/sad minutiae of leaving a home he had grown away from (and probably should never have gone to) and heading out for 'some land I ain't bought...'.

Then there was – same year, same radio programme – *A Nickel For the Fiddler*. The Everly Brothers, in the brief second flowering of their career, released two landmark albums – STORIES WE COULD TELL and PASS THE CHICKEN AND LISTEN – that gave much needed exposure to many of their favourite songwriters. Apart from Guy's song, this was where we first heard tracks like Jesse Winchester's *Brand New Tennessee Waltz* and John Prine's *Paradise*.

These songwriters constructed lyrics in a conversational English as beautiful and succinct as anything Gershwin or Cole Porter ever came up with, and tunes so devastatingly simple and memorable they touched you like sweet recollections of childhood. These were songs to restore your faith in the dignity of man, to keep your dreams afloat. They may at times have danced a little near the edge of sentiment and romanticism, but there was something about the songs that took them well out of country music's mawkish grasp.

That *something* was the use of the language, joyful and thoughtful in equal measure, with the same awareness of sound and rhythm that, in another context, take Raymond Chandler's books way beyond the pulp fiction of the thirties and forties that at first glance they resemble. And there is no-one whose language has given me more joy over the past twentysomething years than Guy Clark.

Jeff Horne

For me it's all about connections. I was introduced to Guy's work (by Jeff) at a time when I had sustained a number of losses in my life and was feeling vulnerable. Discovering Guy Clark's music helped me reconnect to parts of myself that I was thinking had maybe gone for good. It happened this way.

Jeff was playing bass guitar in a six piece band and asked me to try out for the acoustic guitar/vocals vacancy. Guy's songs featured heavily in the band's repertoire. So he compiled a tape for me and I vividly remember as I pressed the play button, I laid down on the sofa, stared at the Marilyn Monroe mirror in my rented room and was poleaxed by the opening line of the song that was playing:

Standing on the gone side of leaving,
She found her thumb and stuck it in the breeze

I didn't hear the rest of the song because somehow that line had freeze-framed me. Being 35 years old, I had been on the gone side of leaving on more than a few occasions and had certainly heard dozens of other songs which cover the theme of relationship endings (I'd even written a couple of fairly forgettable ones myself). But this was different. The frozen frame was allowing me to connect to my own experiences of leaving in a way that made it possible for me to feel the pain, and to be OK with it.

So continued this experience of connection as I embarked on the treasure trail of discovery into Guy Clark's repertoire. Songs that painted vivid pictures which allowed me this access to what I was realising were the shared experiences of another human being – as psychologist Carl Rogers claimed, "what is most personal is most universal."

I'm not sure what it takes to be able to do this: perhaps a deep understanding of one's own self, perhaps an extraordinary gift, perhaps a wealth of personal life experience. Probably all three and a bit more besides. When Guy tells of his experience as a six year old boy in a desolate town in west Texas, turning out to watch the streamline train scream through the countryside, it's not the event itself that I can connect with (as a six year old child I lived in South London where trains were commonplace!), it is more the sense of wonder and the emotional experience contained within.

Unless you live on a desert island, connecting with the experience of fellow human beings is one of the most enriching and broadening parts of personal growth. For this to happen there needs to be people who are brave enough to acknowledge and share with others their own experiences (leaving the individual open to the judgments and attitudes of those less brave) and gifted enough to communicate these experiences in a language that can be understood and interpreted.

They're playing your song, Guy.

Nick Evans

Acknowledgments

THIS book is a totally joint effort: Nick mostly conducted the interviews, and Jeff mostly sorted out which words were relevant and wrote them down in some kind of logical order.

Thanks are due first and foremost to Guy and Susanna Clark for welcoming us into their home and for their support during the writing of the book; and to all the contributors for taking the time to talk to us, particularly Lola Bonner, Keith Case, Travis Clark, Rodney Crowell, Nanci Griffith, Emmylou Harris, Phil Kaufman, Lyle Lovett, Jim McGuire, Holger Petersen, Darrell Scott, Jerry Jeff Walker, Gary B. White, and Miles Wilkinson.

Many thanks also to Richard Wootton and Allan Jones for allowing us to quote from their interviews with Guy and Richard's with Townes Van Zandt; to those who kindly made photographs available; and to all the agents, managers, friends and colleagues who helped in various ways to bring the project together.

Special thanks to Sally, for letting Nick and Jeff swan off to America (just the once!) without her, for helping with the transcriptions, and for looking after Jeff's garden; to Jon for encouragement and advice; and to Neil and Rhia for brightening up our days.

Monahans

Monahans, in Ward County, styles itself 'the Oasis of the West Texas Desert'. The abundant fresh water beneath the sands attracted the Texas and Pacific Railroad, pushing west from Fort Worth in 1881, to select the town as a water stop between the Pecos River and Big Spring.

Guy Charles Clark came into the world in Monahans on November 6, 1941, the first child of Frances and Ellis Clark. It was a month before the Japanese attack on Pearl Harbour which brought America into the Second World War and deprived the growing boy of much of his father's presence during the following years.

For the young Guy Clark, growing up in a small town of just a few thousand people and spending much of his time at his grandmother Rossie's hotel, life revolved around the railroad and the oil wells. The customers of the Clark Hotel, the only one in town, were mainly oilmen working the fields that surrounded Monahans, and they would tell stories that filled a boy's head with wonder; the tales and the experiences would be stored, to be refined and used later in some of his most evocative songs, such as *Texas–1947* and *Desperados Waiting For a Train*. Guy recalls his childhood:

"I was born in Monahans, which is about halfway between Pecos and Odessa, in west Texas. It's very small, and the whole economy was based on oil from the twenties or before. There's some ranching but it takes ten acres to run one cow – that's how sparse the vegetation is, just natural vegetation – so you gotta have a whole lot of land to make it as a rancher.

"Anyway, my grandmother had lived there for years – I don't know when she moved there, probably in the twenties, my father was around seven, I think. They were from Oklahoma. My father's father, they say he was kind of a ne'er-do-well, gambler, all that craziness, but I only saw him once, and he left when my father was still a boy.

"My grandmother was a white-haired, sweet old lady, with one leg – she had her other leg amputated on the kitchen table when she was twelve years old. Running through a cornfield, she got a splinter in her leg, got gangrene. She was pretty tough. And so she just stayed there and raised a kid in this oil boom town and ran a hotel, bootlegging whisky during prohibition.

"I have two younger sisters, each three years apart. This was during World War II – I was born in 1941, so almost from the getgo my father was gone in the service, and then I guess he came back in '46. So for the first five years there was just me and my mother, then two baby sisters, and I never saw my dad except I guess some odd time he'd have a furlough. I went to grade school in Monahans.

"And then the hotel: I was just there a lot, and as I've always said, Jack Prigg – the guy I wrote *Desperados Waiting For a Train* about – was around, he lived there and was just like family. He didn't pay rent and hadn't for years. I don't know how long he lived there, since my father was a kid, I think. He was a friend of my grandmother's, part of the family, like my grandfather. So he's the first male figure I remember. Real cool old guy. He just drilled oil wells, that's what he did all his life."

In an interview with Richard Wootton for the British magazine *Country Music People* in March 1982, Guy again talked about Jack Prigg: "I used to be taken with him everywhere, and I went to the rigs where a very early memory is of a gusher blowing the racking board right out of the derrick – you don't see that sort of thing any more because they have these things much more under control. He took me along to the bars where he hung out, and he taught me a lot about growing up."

One of the incidents that made a lasting impression on Guy was in

Guy Clark's grandmother with Jack Prigg, 1930s (Guy & Susanna Clark collection)

1947 when the first of the big diesel streamline trains started running on the Texas and Pacific line, and the occasion of its first transit through the town became immortalised in what some regard as his finest song, *Texas–1947*. There are very few other songs written with the mixture of wonder, mischief and matter-of-factness that is the authentic voice of a child:

Bein' six years old I had seen some trains before
So it's hard to figure out what I'm at the depot for
Trains are big and black and smokin',
steam screamin' at the wheels
Bigger'n anything there is least that's the way she feels

Trains are big and black and smokin', louder'n July 4
But everybody's actin' like there might be something more
Than just pickin' up the mail or the soldiers from the war
It's something even old man Wileman never seen before

...things got real quiet, and mama jerked me back
But not before I'd got the chance to lay a nickel on the track

"Oh yeah, it's written from that place. I'll never forget it – from the time it happened it was always a memory of mine. And after I wrote that song I played it for my parents and they did not remember it at all. But it happened. It was a big event to go down and see the trains. And that one little detail – about the dime – it's something kids do all over the world. That's not just Texas, *you* did that when you were a kid, everybody's done something like that. It's universal."

The idea of universality comes into the story of Guy Clark's songwriting from the very beginning. It is, after all, difficult to understand how else someone living, for example, five thousand miles away in an alien culture in south London could connect so readily with the songs. The connection is in the detail: you may not recognise the exact circumstance, but you know the feeling behind it. Jerry Jeff Walker, one of the first people to record Guy Clark material and bring it to the attention of the public, tells of the impact Guy's early songs made on him:

"He says things that I wished I'd said – I mean, that's why you choose to write another song. Like with *Desperados Waiting For a Train* – I had a grandfather, he wasn't an oil driller, but he was a country farmer, square dance caller, a very popular man, railroad tracks came through the back of the farm. But there were a lot of things that overlapped there, like him taking me to town when I was a kid. Guy says something that's very clear to you, and you think, I could have written that if that moment would have hit for me.

"I called Guy one night, told him, I said, you know, it's amazing to be doing a 4th July somewheres in Texas, and be playing *Desperados* and have the whole crowd playing and singing the chorus – they've all had an uncle or someone like that in their family. And amazing to have that song in the repertoire and have it – you know, it's really Guy's song, but I did it first – kind of associated with me."

Rockport

Around the turn of the decade, the Clark family moved from Monahans to Rockport, a small city on the Gulf Coast near Corpus Christi, where his father had a law firm. The Clarks were moderately well off, and there was a wide variety of books in the house. Evening poetry readings were a long-standing family tradition and an integral part of home life: Guy mentions authors and poets like Robert Service, Robert Frost and Steven Vincent Benet as influential at this time. But music did not hold a particularly important place in the household:

"I was exposed to a lot of different stuff, art, literature. Both my parents were encouraging in that direction. Painting was something I'd always done, dabbled in it, and they encouraged that too, it's something that's always interested me.

"Neither of my parents could play a radio! They had no interest, they didn't sing, they didn't play any instrument. They were fans of big band music, you know, the music of their youth, swing music, and I suppose whatever they were listening to was the first music I listened to. But we never had a record player until I was a teenager.

"I remember the first time I heard Bill Haley and the Comets do *Rock Around the Clock*. The first 45 single I bought was Little Willie John doing *All Around the World*, the flipside of which was *Fever*.

And also, some of the first records I bought were Louis Armstrong records. This pleased my parents no end, but I really enjoyed it too – it was very cool stuff. I thought Elvis was really good until he got a drummer. I didn't know why, but it's the only music of his I ever liked."

Aside from Guy's parents, there was some musical tradition in the family: his grandmother could play the piano, and on his mother's side, all her mother's brothers and sisters were fiddle players. This part of his family background surfaced later in the song *New Cut Road*, which tells the story behind their trek westward from Kentucky at the end of the last century. But as far as playing music himself went, there was no hint of what was to come until the late 1950s, when he was in high school.

The law firm in Rockport where Ellis Clark worked as an attorney took in as a partner Lola Bonner, a young woman fresh out of college at the University of Texas. She was the first person Guy had known personally who sang and played the guitar. The music she played was Mexican, and he immediately fell in love with it:

"I was absolutely captivated, and actually have been since that day. The music was like the kind of guitars I build now, like mariachi, norteño music. And all the songs were in Spanish, I didn't know any songs in English. There was just something magical about playing the guitar and singing.

"I never was interested in electric guitars, I never wanted one, never had one. But that thing, of sitting and playing and singing, I don't know why, it just knocked me out. And inspired me. I mean, I immediately went to Mexico and got a cheap guitar, and started getting her to show me everything she knew!"

Ms Bonner still practises law in Rockport, and remembers with affection the young Guy Clark:

"We made a trip together when he was a teenager – he went with me to see Señor Andrés Segovia, the classical guitarist of some renown, in Jones Hall in Houston. I thought that was the motivating time for Guy to take up the instrument, not only as an executioner of the instrument but also as a builder.

"At that time I was a partner of his father, that was in '59 and '60 as I best recall, then his father became the county attorney so we dissolved that partnership. I was living in a garage apartment overlooking Aransas Bay. In Rockport we have a barrier island, San José, between us and the Gulf of Mexico. At that time I was employing the use of a classical guitar, but I was playing Mexican music, because the rhythms are absolutely fascinating, and there are two particular rhythms which are 5 and 6 beats or strokes, which employ the use of all of the fingers, much as a classical guitarist, and Guy seemed particularly fascinated with those rhythms, those strokes.

"And I additionally then had all manner of Mexican music on long playing records, and it was just a take – he took to it – which pleased me very much; and later, in a traditional sense, he relied heavily on his upbringing and particularly on his father's ability to narrate stories to the children, relied on those heavily for the content of the various songs he created. So we are extremely proud of him, and I am very grateful for having made an oblique appearance in his life."

Guy continues: "I wasn't writing at this time, just playing the Mexican music she played. I just gravitated toward that one guitar, one voice thing – I mean, I never actually played a song with a drummer till I moved here [to Nashville] and had to do some demos."

Guy visiting Rockport, 1980 (Jim McGuire)

Being inspired by the music wasn't something that normally led to a worthwhile career for a white boy in a middle-class Texas home, and he was still heading towards the typical youthful goals of the time of becoming a doctor, a lawyer, or a jet fighter pilot, and to this end Guy majored in physics at college.

But while these options continued to be available throughout his education – and he knew his parents would have been pleased if he'd followed them up – the feeling of what he actually wanted to do went off in another direction entirely, as the idea of being a folk singer took hold.

Guy says his parents never really resisted the pull – whenever he was ready to go to college and get a real job, they would support him – but it finally became obvious that the lure of folk music was too strong. The evidence was in Guy's attitude:

"I kept flunking out of college! Playing in joints! It was *self*-evident. My parents weren't obstructive about it – as I said, at first they were sure I would get over it, and when I didn't, that was fine."

Apart from music, the other great interest in Guy's life arose from the geographical location of their home. Guy had always loved boats ever since they moved to the coast, and during the summer school holidays in Rockport (and for a year after he left school), he worked in the shipyards as a carpenter's helper, with the last of the men who built the big eighty foot wooden shrimpboats. These were boats constructed to do a job of work, and the experience of being with these men, understanding how they approached the craft of shipbuilding and being part of that fellowship, changed his life.

Much later, songs based on these times flowed from his pen, not only about the shipbuilders and the shrimpers – *South Coast of Texas, Boats To Build, The Carpenter, Blowin' Like a Bandit, Supply and Demand* – but about the dignity of craftsmen and the importance of giving meaning to their work by using it with respect and care. Songs like *Stuff That Works* and *Hanging Your Life on the Wall* demonstrate Guy's deep commitment to the idea that the only way to give true respect to a beautifully crafted object is to use it and not put it in a glass case like a trophy.

Houston

Guy moved to Houston in the early sixties and started playing in the folk clubs in the city. The folk revival was in its heyday, Peter, Paul and Mary were enormously popular, and everyone was doing it. In the traumatic period after President Kennedy's assassination, everybody also seemed to be doing their own bit for the peace effort. Guy was no exception, and had a brief spell in the Peace Corps.

He also became involved in some of the experimental music that was part of the Houston culture at the time with groups like the 13th Floor Elevators; he very briefly joined the first incarnation of Mayo Thompson's free-form psychedelic band The Red Crayola, and contributed photographs to album covers for International Artists, one of the more prominent local independent labels. During this period he formed a folk trio with Kay Oslin and David Jones, but it didn't last very long. For Guy Clark it was fun to sing and play with two other folk musicians, and even though it may have lasted only a few gigs, it formed part of his musical education. The trio played the typical folk music of the era, covering songs by groups like The Weavers and arrangements of traditional whaling songs, murder ballads and so on. But the notion of writing songs hadn't really entered Guy's head, and it wasn't until the late sixties that it did.

He was still performing solo in clubs, playing mainly traditional folk music, when he began to meet up with several musicians who seemed to have the same attitude towards life and music. These included Mickey Newbury, Jerry Jeff Walker, Townes Van Zandt, and Gary B. White.

Gary recalls the events and circumstances that led to them eventually becoming roommates: "I was at the University of Texas in 1961, doing engineering, but mostly playing music like the Kingston Trio, the Weavers, Pete Seeger. I dropped out of school and went in the army for three years. While I was over in Korea a friend sent me a tape of what they were currently listening to in Austin, Texas, and it turned out to be the New Lost City Ramblers and Ewan MacColl and Peggy Seeger and a new guy, Bob Dylan. I didn't have much to do, but I had my guitar, you know, so I would listen to tapes and brush up on my guitar playing.

"When I got back, Bob Dylan had just released his second album, it had *Don't Think Twice* on it, and I was listening to the picking on that particular record and I said, gee, it's so much like Elizabeth Cotton's style of playing, and I liked that finger-picking style, so I kinda taught myself. Well, when I came out of the army in 1964 I returned to Houston.

"I never knew Guy up to that time, but a friend of mine there informed me there was a club out on the Westheimer Road called the Jesters Cabaret where people were playing live folk music and they were selling beer, and it would be a good place. I hadn't determined at that point whether I was amateur or better, but they had open mike nights and people hanging around, so I began to go out there, and that's when I first bumped into Guy – out in the parking lot of the Jesters.

"The dressing room was where they stored all the beer kegs and it was quite small, it was more of a storage room, so the entertainers at that time would sorta flow over out into the parking lot – especially in Texas it would be nice on a summer evening, you know, it was pretty hot and if you weren't in the air conditioned part of the club, well you didn't want to be back in that stuffy old dressing room. Another couple that was playing at the club at that time, a local couple from Houston, was called Frank and Kay – Frank Davis and Kay Oslin, who later became K.T. Oslin. There was a lot of talent there.

"So Guy and I were shuffling around out in the parking lot and I was showing him this picking style that I'd learned, taught myself, and Guy said, man that's great, we gotta do this. So I was teaching him some of that, and as we got talking he said, where are you staying? Well, I just got out of the army so I rented myself a single place, an apartment, you know – after living in an army hut with 32 guys I was kinda enjoying being alone – and he said, you know what, if we pooled our resources we could actually rent a whole big house, and we'd each have a bedroom, a private room, and he said, I'm going to start repairing guitars and I need a work area. Guy had come to town with an old friend of his from Rockport, Carl Snyder, but Carl had got married so Guy needed a roommate, he couldn't quite make all the rent on his own. He seemed a nice enough person, so I said, let's do that.

"So we shopped around in the old part of Houston and found a house, half a house at least, a huge two storey, the upstairs was a separate apartment. We took this place with a couple of bedrooms and a sleeping porch Guy could use for his guitar repair shop, and he stocked it up with tools, and he started just doing wonderful work with his hands. He's a craftsman in so many ways, and it shows in his songs, they almost reflect a quality about his craftsmanship and you can tell he is a guy that's at home in a wood shop or working with his hands.

"We lived in that place for about a year, and went out and worked in clubs. Another club had opened called the Sand Mountain Coffee House on Richmond, and at that time Jerry Jeff Walker had started coming around town, he had been playing down in New Orleans. Guy and I were just simply outgrowing this duplex we were living in; Guy had met up with another guitar repair fellow, Minor Wilson from Austin, Texas, and what they wanted to do was open a guitar shop together and look at building guitars.

"So we found a place on Fannin Street where we could get the whole house and Guy and I rented the upstairs where we lived – the house was so old it still had working gaslights in it – but downstairs Minor Wilson and Guy would have a guitar shop. They decided they were going to build a guitar, which they did, they built a very beautiful 12-string. They had the bathtub downstairs filled with water and pieces of wood soaking in the water, so that they could bend it properly – in order to bend the sides of the guitar you have to wet the wood through so that you can warp it in some die blocks that hold its shape – so they were doing that, and I'd been in electronics in the army so I did the occasional amplifier repair for them."

The Sand Mountain Coffee House was a family business owned by a woman called Mrs Carrick, who took advantage of the sixties folk boom, and the fact that the audiences it attracted were not the usual rowdy rock crowds, to run a folk club. Jerry Jeff Walker remembers:

"Townes [Van Zandt] and I were playing there and Guy was actually, I guess the word would be touring, or at least getting gigs out of town, whereas most of us stayed around town. But I just remember the first time seeing Guy perform, I thought he really knew what he was doing. He sang and played – he didn't write – a lot of traditional stuff. In fact the first time I saw him he was in something like a suit coat – I guess he played other gigs where he had to dress up more! Anyway, there was something about him that made him look to me more professional than us in the sense of his stage presence – more than Townes and I.

"Some people make you feel very comfortable right away, and some make you uneasy. I try to tell people, don't apologise for your inadequacies, the audience doesn't need to know that. I read a quote one time that an artist's job is to make his art look easy – he doesn't bring the labour to the stage. That's why they've always said, oh he must be born with all this talent, you know, but the artist practices his ass off, so he doesn't make it look laborious when he does it. And Guy has this maturity and something special about him. I can't tell you how long he'd been on stage and playing, but that was the first time that I saw him, and where we linked up is that Townes and I in our own clumsy way hadn't learned to perform that well, but we were *writing*.

"Roger Miller once told me that, from his point of view, if you learn someone else's song and perform it, everybody knows it and they can compare you to them; but if you write your own and play it, there's no way to compare that, so your security lies in the fact that it's your own and there's no comparison. You know, someone may come along and do your song better, but in the meantime there's no way to compare it to, say, a hit version.

"So we were kind of going in that direction, I think we were taking the tradition and we were adding our own stuff to it, and that interested Guy. And that was kind of our overlap – he would say, how do you guys do that? and we'd go, because we can't learn the traditional ones as good as you can – Guy could really learn them the right way."

Gary B. White continues the story: "Guy had met Susan, who became his first wife, about that time, and Jerry Jeff had decided that whenever he came to town our sofa would be a good place for him to hang his hat, so he kinda got to staying with us and the three of us would sit around and play a lot, go out to the coffee house or the Jesters and play our music. The only one writing at this time was Jerry Jeff and he'd just written his song *Mr Bojangles*, and we were all sort of impressed with that, but we were thinking we were just a couple of knockabout guitar players, guys like us can't write!

"So anyway, the last year I was in Houston, which was about 1965 or '66, Guy and Susan got married and later they had their first son, I guess their only son, Travis. Guy was still staying downstairs with the guitar shop and building his guitars, doing guitar repairs, but he moved in with Susan and I didn't want to stay there and Jerry Jeff didn't look like he wanted to pick up half the rent, and by then he'd moved his whole band in! So I said, I'm taking a small apartment again by myself, I've had it, I feel like I'm back in the barracks. So they kinda took over the whole apartment – Jerry Jeff, Bob Bruno and Pete Troutner – and I guess they stayed there rent-free till the landlord kicked them out!

"So they ran off to New York and failed, got their instruments stolen, so Jerry Jeff ended up back in Texas, at which time he asked me – I was playing bass and singing in this band the Baroque Brothers, had an electric guitar and some amplifiers and stuff – Jerry Jeff says, hey why don't you come to New York and be in our band, and I said, yeah, let's do it. I told Guy and he said, well, we're going to close down the shop pretty soon. I'd given up my job in aerospace, I was 26 years old, so I just said, let's go!"

The guitar shop was in fact closed down, and Minor Wilson, Guy's partner, moved to San Francisco, where he eventually opened another one in the North Beach area of the city.

Guy was listening to other Texas folk and blues musicians such as John Lomax, Mance Lipscomb and Lightnin' Hopkins at this time, and his guitar playing was strongly influenced by this new element, but more importantly the idea of singing his own songs started to take hold:

"I got turned on to writing through Townes and Jerry Jeff. Townes had just started writing, a couple or so songs when I first met him. And Jerry Jeff – I met them just playing folk clubs in Houston. Townes lived there, and Jerry Jeff did intermittently. There were a couple of clubs there in the sixties where folk music was played. Anyway, Townes had started writing and I had never really tried to, I suppose I was content singing traditional folk music and the odd Bob Dylan song. But Townes was the first person I really heard write anything – and like I said, it was only his first or second song – that was more than just rhyming moon, June and spoon or I'm a ramblin'

Guy in guitar workshop, San Francisco, 1969 (Guy & Susanna Clark collection)

kind of guy. It was very literate, intelligent, passionate work.

"And just like the same way I went for playing the guitar the first time I saw it done, the first time I heard anybody write like that, that was it, it became do-able. Jerry's a great inspiration too – I've known him forever and is a dear, dear friend."

So Guy Clark started writing songs, in a hardcover exercise book that he has to this day, and continued playing and singing, solo or with his friends, around Texas.

In 1969 Guy and Susan were divorced, and he moved to San Francisco, where he rejoined Minor Wilson in his guitar repair shop and continued to write and to play in the city's clubs. "I just went out there to get away from Texas," he says, "to see what was going on in the world."

The Summer of Love in San Francisco had by this time turned into a winter of discontent, and The City lost its attraction. Returning to Texas, Guy's interest in art and photography eventually led him to a job as art director of a CBS affiliated television station in Houston, where he worked for about a year. And met Susanna (but we'll let Susanna tell that story later).

Finally around 1970, coming up to thirty years of age, he had to make the decision, if he was not going to wish he had done it for the rest of his life, to try and make music – writing songs and playing them – his life, rather than be an art director. So, with the encouragement of Susanna and her presence by his side, he quit the television station and moved again to California – this time to Los Angeles.

Long Beach

The move to southern California was crucial to, and the effects resonated throughout, the course of Guy Clark's career.

"Susanna and I went out to California," he says, "with a batch of songs that I no longer play, to get seriously into the music business, as opposed to it being an avocation. And we found a house in Long Beach. I worked in the Dobro factory, building Dobros all day, and when I could make an appointment with somebody, I would take my guitar into Los Angeles – I didn't have any demo tapes – and sit and play them till they'd say yes or no.

"And did that for about eight months until I finally met the head of RCA's publishing company, a guy named Gerry Teifer. I played him four songs and he just said, that's good, he said how much money do you want and where do you want to live? It was just like – bingo! They had offices in Nashville, LA, and New York, and I could be wherever I wanted. I did not particularly like LA, simply because it's just so big and so hard to get around and it's very cliquish. I knew one person here in Nashville, Mickey Newbury, who I'd met through Townes. He was encouraging, so we subsequently, within a week or two, moved to Nashville with a songwriting deal."

In a 1978 interview with Allan Jones for *Melody Maker*, Guy elaborated on the circumstances: "I didn't know how long I might have to hold out for a deal, but I was patient. I was prepared to wait. I was real determined. At some point in your life you gotta make a decision about what you're gonna do. I didn't wanna wake up 40 years old saying, 'We-e-ell, I wish I'd done that.' I was determined to do it. So I got on with it."

And the reason for choosing Nashville? "It's a better place to do business," he explained. "The whole music business is concentrated in one area, just about. It's really no problem to do business. You just walk across the street. It's not like Los Angeles where to get into a building to see someone you have to get through two secretaries and four armed guards. In Nashville, if you wanna see Chet Atkins, you just go see him."

Gary B. White still lives near Los Angeles with his wife Annie, but at the time hadn't seen much of Guy for a few years. He describes his reaction to hearing Guy's songs for the first time: "I moved from New York, my wife and I moved out to Los Angeles in 1970, and we got a telephone call. It was Guy, and he said, I didn't know you were living out here, and I said, I didn't know you were here either, and I said, gosh, that's great, you know, I gotta get down to see you, and he said, well you better do it soon because I'm leaving in two days to go to Nashville! So we tore down there and spent the evening together.

"It was sort of like finding out that your brother or sister is talented in a way that you didn't know, it's more just an oddity, I really didn't think about it much at the time. I just took it for granted that of course he can do this, he's Guy Clark, and of course I can write a song and I don't think he was surprised that I was capable of writing either. It was kind of the original glue that held us together. I must say that I haven't lived with other people that much – except my wife for thirty years and the guys in the army! – but Guy Clark was a very very easy person to live with, he was considerate of you and we got on fabulously. We both had a respect for each other's privacy, but we could be good friends to each other too, so in a way I didn't have this immediate reaction that I was bowled over by what he was doing, it was just Guy except it was on paper.

"Guy for me is just Guy, you know. I knew him first as Guy, the fellow I lived with for two years, we were very close and we sat and played guitars together, so it just seems like his work, everything he does is just a logical extension of the man himself. At least we shared those musical roots, we sat in the same living room listening to the same records. Sometimes I think I had more of an ear for changes, for hearing things, taking something off a record. Sometimes Guy would ask me, what is he doing, how is he playing that guitar part, and I had an ear for that, but we all have different facets and Guy manifests his in different ways, his lyrics are brilliant. I don't want to just give way to accolades – not that he doesn't deserve them – but it's just not the way we see each other, it's just what I expected of him."

The Long Beach period, brief though it was, turned out to be very constructive. Guy had been continuing to write songs in his little exercise book, as well as playing in an acoustic bluegrass band, and it was during this time that he finally wrote a song he considered good enough to keep as a complete work. The song was *That Old Time Feeling*:

"That was the first one I wrote that I still sing. It was the first one that when I wrote it I knew it was a good song – and all the rest of the things I'd written made no difference. This was the one I knew was real good, that made me realise I could do it."

Darrell Scott, the guitarist who appears on Guy's two most recent albums, adds a younger man's perspective on the song, which he regards as one of his favourites: "It's so hard to just pick one song above the others, but I really respond to *Old Time Feeling*, that's a pretty high standard! To me, it's such a piece of writing, just a camera taking shots of the humanity, whether it's the old soldiers or the girl with the clear blue eyes, I mean everything is just a little snapshot that builds to this vibe and this mood – you feel like you're wearing a coat of all those themes at the end of a song like that."

All the time that songs were being written, notice was being taken of the people and things Guy came into contact with, and snippets and phrases were being noted, usually by writing it onto a bar napkin (Guy has one pinned on the wall of his workshop with his favourite epigram, dedicated to Susanna, written on it: 'My life was a blank napkin until I met you'). The germ of his best-known early song, *LA Freeway*, came from this period, even though the song itself, according to Guy, was written later:

Skinny Dennis Sanchez, Los Angeles, c.1970 (Guy & Susanna Clark collection)

"I was playing in a little string band, just some people in Long Beach playing traditional music. Skinny Dennis was the bass player, and a man and wife, or boyfriend and girlfriend, played banjo and fiddle. We were playing one night in San Diego, and about four o'clock in the morning we were driving back north to Long Beach.

"About halfway there I'd fallen asleep in the back of this car, and I just kinda raised up and I looked around, and I said, man, if I can just get off this LA freeway without getting killed or caught. A light bulb went off, and I borrowed an eyebrow pencil from Susanna and a burger bag, and wrote it down, and put the scrap of paper in my wallet and carried it for about a year – not quite a year, maybe – or so. I wrote that song after we moved to Nashville.

"You couldn't write that song if you were in the middle of it, you had to do it with perspective. But I kept it because it was *good*. I mean, I didn't know what the song was going to be about or what it was. That's why those little snippets, when you think of something, are important – if you don't write it down in the context, you won't remember it. And that one I did. And that instance is actually what taught me to do that, to say, this is a valuable discipline; make yourself do this.

"And it's the first song that got any attention – Jerry Jeff did it – yeah, it was a very important song. I still do it."

Townes Van Zandt, in an interview with Richard Wootton for *Omaha Rainbow* magazine in 1977, gave his own angle on his early days with Guy:

"I guess I met Guy Clark a couple of years after I started playing. He was at the Jesters before I played there and then joined the Peace Corps. I started playing there and then he came back, we met, and we've been good friends ever since.

"Skinny Dennis met Guy when Guy came out to California to get his publishing deal together. Guy was real serious, real conscientious about it, and to support himself while looking for the deal he worked at the Dobro factory, and also in a bluegrass group that came together in Long Beach. I can't remember if they were called anything, but it was a trio. Guy played rhythm guitar and sang, another guy played banjo, and Skinny Dennis played stand-up bass. Long Beach is real heavy duty. It has all the disadvantages of Los Angeles and none of the advantages, a real crazy place.

"So Dennis became good friends with Guy, and Guy from there moved to Nashville. The group kind of split up because the banjo player thought Guy and Dennis were too rowdy. He once made the comment that the only reason they played was for an excuse to drink. Guy said, 'Man, I don't need no excuse to drink!' So the group fell apart. Guy got his deal and moved to Nashville, then six months later Dennis decided he would follow suit. They were living in Nashville for, I guess, a year and a half."

NASHVILLE

GUY and Susanna arrived in Nashville in 1971 with a bookful of Guy's songs for his publishing company, Sunbury Music, to pitch to the record companies. There was no deal for a certain number of new songs, it was just whatever he wrote. The first one that was recorded was a talking blues called *The Old Mother's Locket Trick* by Harold Lee on Cartwheel Records (also cut later by Waylon Jennings), but the most important early sign of recognition was when *A Nickel for the Fiddler* was taken up; Mickey Newbury had introduced Guy to the Everly Brothers, themselves RCA artists at the time, and they cut the song for their 1972 album PASS THE CHICKEN AND LISTEN. Unexpectedly, Guy got to play on the Chet Atkins-produced album:

"I was there when they were recording it, and Chet was listening to the demo – it's kind of frailing the guitar with the back of your nails, like you frail a banjo, in an open G tuning, and Chet could not figure out how to play it. None of the guitar players could figure out how to play it, so he turned to the whole studio and said, do you mind if Guy comes and plays this on this record, because none of us can play it, and he's not in the union, so don't anybody tell! Everybody said yeah, fine. So it's actually me playing on that Everly Brothers Record."

A Nickel For the Fiddler was part of the batch of early songs that eventually made it on to Guy's first album, but it's one he no longer plays:

"I still don't do the song, simply because I wrote it in a strange tuning, with a strange way to play it, and I've never been able to figure out how to make it sound the same without retuning, which I refuse to do on stage anymore. Every once in a while I do try to relearn to play that song on guitar, but I just can't make it sound as good as the original."

The difficulties of a rookie songwriter trying to get his songs heard by the Nashville establishment were considerable, as Guy explained to Allan Jones in 1978 – with the added perspective of six years' hindsight:

"I wouldn't go so far as to say they were suspicious, or actively tried to resist the changes that were taking place. They just didn't understand a lot of the new things that were happening. I mean, they didn't understand my songs. They were a little more complex lyrically than most of the things they'd heard. Consequently, most of the producers, who were just lookin' for hit songs, didn't wanna know at first. You gotta accept that, though. This is a business. We're all trying to make a little money, you know. This ain't a charity. So if you wanna write ten minute songs, fine. Great. But that's not what they want. So don't bitch.

"And I'm beginning to realise that you can write more effectively within the discipline of a two- or three-minute song. Slowly, I'm becoming more concise. I don't think it's a compromise. My songs are just naturally becoming less complex, which I like. I think I've gone through a period of writing complex, involved songs like *The Last Gunfighter Ballad*. That's a beautiful song, and I'm very proud to have written it. But you can't write like that forever. If only because it would turn into a formula.

"There's more tolerance [now], but still you get people sayin' that some of the things that I do and that Townes does isn't country music. But it's a lot closer to country music than a lot of the things that are being made into hit records by country stations. I don't mean to put any of that down. It has a place, you know. But Ronnie Milsap is not a country singer. He's a rhythm and blues piano player who learned how to do that when he realised there was a market for a blind piano-playing country singer. Fine. I'm sure he loves the music and the success. But Townes is a lot closer to country music than that."

Susanna Clark, later in the book, gives a vivid picture of what it was like in their early days in Nashville. Their best friend from Houston, Townes Van Zandt, stayed on and off at their various homes, and there was an enormous amount of mutual support between them and the other writers in their group, including Newbury, Walker, and, a little later, Rodney Crowell. Guy told Richard Wootton in 1982 about them and about some of the difficulties in finding places to play:

"Rodney is superb, and Townes is the best as far as I'm concerned. He was the best man at our wedding, which was a crazy affair! About the only place that we could play was the Exit/In, a tiny club where they had 'Writers' Nights' on Mondays or Tuesdays and where you could show off your songs and meet other writers. A lot of people helped to get the songs around, like Mickey Newbury and Jerry Jeff Walker, who was an old friend. He came through town and hung out for a couple of days and listened to what I was doing, and wound up recording *LA Freeway*."

Jerry Jeff explains the circumstances behind this:

"I flew up to Nashville to visit Jimmy Buffet, found out Guy was living on Chapel Street and called over, I think Keith Sykes was there also. I remember going over to the house to visit and we were all kind of glad to be reunited. I told them I was staying for a while and Guy said, you know what, I've written something. I said, what'd you write, and he played me *That Old Time Feeling*, and I thought, that's pretty damn good! But it didn't faze me that much because he knew so much about songs and knew good songs from bad songs, and that was good. So that was the first one, and then he also said that the day he wrote that, he brought it down and played it for some friends, and they liked it so well he went back upstairs and wrote some more!

"The thing about writing a song, of course, is to give it a timeless feel, like it could have been something written a hundred years ago or yesterday. And *Old Time Feeling* has that, in its simplicity of melody and simplicity of lyrics. As Billy Joe Shaver used to say, there's no wasted words – it's kind of whittled down to the essence of it. That makes it special.

"So I decided to record *Old Time Feeling* and I went to New York shortly thereafter to do my Jerry Jeff Walker album. I was just about to go to the studio, I'd been up all night, drinking or something, I was still cramming, trying to figure out the song – and I called Guy to ask him, how does it go, so he had to recite the lyrics to me over the phone, because I was going into this studio in a few hours as long as I didn't fall asleep, you know, and so we crammed that at the last minute.

"And then in my song *Pissing In the Wind*, I make reference to that: 'Well I called this guy, it was four in the morning, he'd read the words to the song we were singing,' so that's kind of how I got it. Because I always kind of let songs come to me, I didn't immediately say right then the day he played it, that's great, I'm going to record it – I went, that's good, I like that; then I was going down the road somewheres and I'd think, that's pretty neat, and I'd think about it for a while, and then I might play what I can remember of it at a

Susanna and Guy on tour, early 1970s (Guy & Susanna Clark collection)

party, and that's how it becomes my song, and my own remembrance of how it went is how I do it. That's sort of how the arrangement comes. And then I call him back and put all the pieces back in, and then sometimes I even have to correct myself – oh yeah, that's how you were doing it, I thought it was this way. So it's my arrangement by osmosis, then I have to kind of clean up the edges a little bit.

"Anyway, I told them in New York one of the songs I was going to do was *Old Time Feeling*. I played it for a bunch of people in my office and they kind of went, yeah, okay, and I said, you ought to be looking at signing this guy Guy Clark, he's a good musician and he's writing a lot. They said, well, what else has he written? All I could remember was the first verse and chorus of 'Pack up all your dishes', but I just went and kind of played it, and they went, *that's* the one – you gotta do that one on the record. And I said okay, I'll do both of them!

"In the studio, when you're mixing everything or someone says, we need to do the guitar part again on that 'LA Freeway' song, you kinda start knowing which one it is because they keep calling it that. Well as Guy said, when we were young, the first line we ever wrote for a song was what we started calling it, but the idea is to find whatever you repeat in the song and then you say it over and over and that's what gets hooked in people's minds. I've had people come up to me and say, do that song that has that thing about the tree in it, and a park, and I wouldn't know what the hell they wanted – oh, *Mr Bojangles*, right! It's got a tree somewhere mentioned in it! Something kinda sticks out in their mind and that's how they remember it.

"Anyway, 'LA Freeway' was what they kept saying, so I just called him and said if we're going to title it, why don't we just title it by what everybody's calling it, and he said, fine, I don't care! So I recorded both of them, and *LA Freeway* was the single – they were right!"

Guy adds: "I first titled it 'Pack Up All Your Dishes'; the actual copyright is 'LA Freeway (Pack Up All Your Dishes)'. So I quit naming songs and just waited until someone said, hey, here's what it is!"

LA Freeway illustrates how Guy Clark's approach to writing varies from song to song: "It's never the same, I don't have a formula. Sometimes it's a bar napkin, or something I've written down and put in my wallet, sometimes it's a guitar piece, which is actually how *LA*

Freeway started up. I had the melody first, that little guitar lick, and then I put the words of the verse to that. I've written whole songs and never picked up a guitar, just written it all out because that part of the juices – the words and the rhymes – was flowing and to confuse it with trying to put music to it at that point would be silly."

Jerry Jeff Walker's next album, VIVA TERLINGUA in 1973, also included one of Guy's songs, *Desperados Waiting For a Train*. Jerry Jeff explains how he came to play the song for the first time:

"This was one of the real weird ones. The first time Guy came to play in Austin, I wanted to get a crowd for him, he hadn't played there yet, so I announced that I would play that evening to guarantee a crowd, and I sort of said it would be a freebie, and when Guy got to town we stayed up all night, got real drunk.

"And Guy had to go open the show – he was tired, but he went down and opened, while I stayed home and made a few more drinks in the blender. I came to town in cowboy boots, cutoff shorts, tee shirt, cowboy hat and my dog, and I played about two songs and passed out! So Guy got up and played while I just lay there in the corner! All of a sudden I woke up, he was doing a song, I remember, and I got up and sang harmony on it. And then we left!

"So the next weekend I said I would come back and make up for everybody, and I didn't want to ask my band to come because I thought they were mad at me. And on the night, it was just about half an hour before the show, one by one they came walking through the door and they said, let's play, and we played one of the best sets we ever played. And in honour of Guy it was the first time I ever tried out *Desperados* and it got a standing ovation. It kind of says something good, or something about the loyalty of the band... well, everybody falls down once in a while, you just gotta make sure you get back up."

Although the subject matter goes back to Guy's childhood in Monahans, the writing of the song also dates from Guy and Susanna's spell in Los Angeles; the pleasure in the achievement has stayed with him through the years and is obvious when he talks about it now:

"I wrote that in Long Beach one Saturday afternoon. I was off work, just having the best time in the world, drinkin' wine, and wrote that song. And I was ec*stat*ic! And I played it for Susanna and she said, how can you be so happy about such a sad song? I said, no, no, you don't understand, it's not the song, it's the *fact* that it's a song."

In 1974 the rock journalist Jan Reid wrote the seminal book on Texas culture and music, *The Improbable Rise of Redneck Rock*, with particular reference to Austin. Originally published by Heidelberg Publishers in Austin itself, the book sweeps across the cultural landscape from Larry McMurtry to Willie Nelson, taking in lesser-known names like Willis Alan Ramsey and Michael Murphy, and includes a chapter on the music and excesses of Jerry Jeff Walker.

This chapter contains the first mention, certainly in book form, of Guy Clark: the reference is to Jerry Jeff's initial recordings at Austin's Odyssey Studio for his first MCA album and to and to 'a couple of borrowed songs that seemed specifically written for [him].' About *That Old Time Feeling* Reid noted that it was 'as moody and downhearted as anything Walker ever wrote,' and about *LA Freeway*, 'The lyrics were both a surrender and a beginning, a nightmarish awakening from the American dream of moving ever westward. Instrumentally, the cut was a jangling clash of the cultural influences on Austin music: a long-haired Teamster crazed by too much speed and too little sex, too stoned to move but in a hurry to get home. And while any Depression Okie could identify with the lyrics, so could any freak who had ever made the mistake of driving an automobile under the influence of LSD.'

There is a feeling, which Gary B. White previously noted, of Guy Clark's talent, even at this early stage in his career, being taken almost for granted. Writing about VIVA TERLINGUA, Reid says, almost in passing, that *Desperados* is 'the best cut on the album,' and Bill C. Malone in his influential *Country Music USA* blithely called Clark 'the best songwriter to drift through Austin.'

August 1972 had seen the arrival in Nashville from Houston of a young singer who was to be a part of Guy and Susanna Clark's life on and off from that time. Rodney Crowell blew into town with his friend Donivan Cowart. Rodney recalls the first, somewhat unpromising, meeting with Guy: "Donivan and I were at college together, we were college roommates, we wrote songs together, goofed off, and we came to Nashville together with a guy named Chris

Grooms. I remember when I first got here, people said to me, you gotta meet Guy Clark, you know, he's the guy. I was living in my car for a while and finally I got a house over in the Hillsborough Village area with a couple of rounders, Skinny Dennis Sanchez and Richard Dobson – the three of us had a house that was just kind of the stopover place for all of the itinerant musicians and folksingers and such. That's when I first met Guy and Susanna, I came in one day and they were there.

"My first impression of Guy was that he was passed out on my bed! All I saw was this pair of rough cowboy boots hanging off the end of the bed, just a tall guy passed out – I actually started talking to Susanna first, I guess I got to know Susanna a little more quickly than Guy, but we eventually got to know each other pretty well.

"The kind of street level Texas singer songwriter society that was here in Nashville, the folk singers, alternative songwriters, Guy was kind of the hub of it, a lot of it revolved around him, he was really solid. The prince of it all was Townes Van Zandt, who was usually on the road, or breezing in and out. He was kind of a ramblin' Jack guy, but Guy was kind of the staple that held it all down.

"He's extremely intelligent, you know, and just a compelling figure, a tall, dark, very charismatic character who was just a brilliant writer, really an F. Scott [Fitzgerald] kind of guy. The thing about it was, in the early days Guy was the person who I had access to and a real relationship with, somebody I hung with who was a friend, who was really an artist functioning up to his potential. I was young and impressionable, and Guy more than anybody was the songwriter who introduced me to the craft of writing songs. I was young when I got here, I wasn't writing really good stuff, and it was really due to Guy and Townes and Mickey Newbury that I started to understand that there was a higher stake in the game, you know, and Guy was just on the streets with it."

Skinny Dennis Sanchez is a figure that flits in and out of the early Guy Clark story, and is immortalised in a whole verse of *LA Freeway* ('the only one I think I will miss'). He died in October 1972, and Townes, in his interview with Richard Wootton, told a story (which Susanna later corroborated) of Dennis visiting the Clarks' house after he died:

"The only people there were Susanna and I. We were talking about Dennis, and this was the year after that song and it was Christmas, so it was December. All of a sudden, without any wind or anything else, the screen door opened. It was the middle of the night, one or two o'clock. To open, the latch had to turn. The latch turned, the screen door opened about this far, and then closed. My wife had already gone to bed, so had Guy; Susanna and I were just talking about Dennis and that happened. We made a little joke about it being Dennis. Said, 'Why don't you take a seat Dennis?' Pointed to the rocking chair, and the rocking chair moved! Then my hair just went whew!!! Then Susanna said, 'Well, Dennis, it's real good to have you visit, but there's no extra beds. I guess you'll have to go sleep in the car.' The rocking chair went again, the door opened...

"Susanna and I were both stone sober. The first night Cindy and I arrived the four of us had stayed up and talked all night. This was the second night, and you know how if you have a few drinks over a period of time you get real sober. That's the condition we were in and we both saw it, both saw all that happened, and I just kind of blew it. I don't think about it."

Evenings around this time saw the friends gathering together at one or other of their houses, forming a kind of songwriters' circle, trading songs and guitar licks back and forth. Rodney Crowell, as one of the younger participants, sometimes felt in awe of the others:

"Back then, before we all had responsibilities, going on the road, performing or producing records or doing all that, mainly I would go off and write songs so that we could all get together and play our songs for each other, and my goal was to write something good enough in one of these late night circle of songwriters to have it recognised as being okay, as having done something. I remember very specifically the first time that I played a song to Guy and Townes where Guy kinda nodded and said, that's okay, man, and from there, once that happened I personally started to be able to tap in to my talent, or to combine craft with talent.

"I never had any competition with Guy or Susanna, but I was certainly in competition with Townes Van Zandt. Townes was just brilliant, you know, but I think the competition for all of us was for Guy's attention and approval, and I think when Guy started to really warm up to me and when we started to get close, Townes and I became sort of competitive with each other, because Townes was really Guy's best friend, and I was just a new kid come lately who they took a fancy to and kinda opened up to me."

Phil Kaufman is one of the true legends of contemporary music. He it was who stole the body of his friend Gram Parsons, in a pact made at Clarence White's funeral a few months before Parsons died, and took it out to the Joshua Tree National Monument in the Mojave desert to cremate it. Since that time he has been the road manager of a score of acts from Elizabeth Ashley to Frank Zappa, but is probably best known for looking after Emmylou Harris on her road trips for the last 25 years.

He and Guy are old friends; when we were talking with Guy in the hospitality room after his Waterman's Centre gig in London this year, he saw Phil coming through the door and hugged him like a long-lost brother. Phil puts another perspective on the Guy/Susanna/ Townes/Rodney group:

"All those guys who came up together, you don't wanna drink with them! Rodney's a lightweight, you can drink with Rodney – Rodney learned early! But I mean, you sit down at a bar with Guy, Townes, Susanna and Rodney, Rodney'll drive you home! The rest of us'll say thank you Rodney the next morning. How did we get home? – it was Rodney. Rodney learned early that you don't need to be drunk to write a country song, you only need a pen. But Guy had a great constitution, still does, he's a big guy and he can do it, you know, when he wants to."

On a wall in the Clarks' house, there is a framed pair of photographs from the early 1970s of Rodney and Guy holding airguns and bits of glass, looking very pleased with themselves. Rodney explains: "Guy and Susanna were thinking about leaving, moving out of their house [in East Nashville], so they took all of their crystal and wine glasses and stuff and stacked them outside. Guy and I had these BB guns we were playing with at the time, and we set up all of that glassware and said, okay, one shot per glass, and at the end it'll be a piece of sculpture!"

Susanna adds: "The story is that it was all of our dishes, and we

Rodney & Guy with BB guns and trophies, c.1973 (Susanna Clark)

didn't want to pack the dishes when we moved, so we just decided to shoot them!"

"And at the end of it," continues Rodney, "at the very last, there was one tall wine goblet still standing, and Guy said, well I got one shot left, and he shot from his hip and shot the stem of that wine glass perfectly, with the top of the glass just settled right beside it. A magic shot! I think that was my favourite collaboration I ever had with Guy, and my favourite photograph!"

Old No. 1

When they moved to Nashville, Guy had every intention of trying to record his own songs himself at some time, but the first step was the songwriting deal. Over the next couple of years, a few more of Guy's songs were sold to other artists, but gradually the priority slid across to making an album of his own. Finally in 1975 it happened. Sunbury Music was RCA's publishing company, and through meeting people in the company and playing them the songs, and them hearing the demos he had been making, Guy got a record deal with RCA.

"I think Chet Atkins was probably instrumental in that; being the figurehead he was at RCA, he was very helpful in doing something as off the wall as that was at the time, that far from mainstream country. He was very supportive."

The resulting album was Old No. 1, one of the most stunning sets of original songs anyone in the American folk/country scene had ever heard.

"One of the things is, with your first album, you have a ton of songs to choose from, and you glean the best ten out of fifty, maybe, or twenty, whatever, but you get to pick the best ten. And that never happens again, ever!

"I mean, a lot of those songs I wouldn't write today, even though they were passionate and heartfelt at the time. I don't feel like that now – I'm dumber and I'm older. Which doesn't mean that they're not good songs. Some of them I can do, and some of them I can't.

"I go back and forth with a song called *Like a Coat From The Cold,* for example. People use it at their weddings, they love it, I get requests for it, but if you sit down and listen to that song, what a self-serving asshole I must have been to write, 'the woman I have chosen' – I have chosen, to walk through my life! Like a coat – I mean, where the fuck is that coming from! I wouldn't write that today – if you look at it like that, that's a very kind of, not necessarily sexist, but self-involved position. I would not write it today, and consequently I sometimes have a hard time doing it. I can't get my head the right distance from it."

Guy's personal favourite among his own songs is another of the album's highlights. On stage, he sometimes describes *She Ain't Goin' Nowhere* as "ten seconds in a woman's life." It opens with the defiant lines:

Standin' on the gone side of leavin'
She found her thumb and stuck it in the breeze
She'll take anything that's goin' close to somewhere
She can lay it down or live it like she'd please

"One of the reasons that song's my favourite is because it happened like *(snaps his fingers)* that. Forty five minutes, it just wrote itself – I didn't rework it, I didn't edit it, and it was just this image I had. I mean surely it's somethin' about Susanna, just her character, not the actual thing that's going on, but just the character of the woman – it's that look, right there, that says fuck you, I ain't scared of nothin'! I'm not going anywhere, I'm leavin'.

"I grew up around really strong women, women who were not namby-pamby housewives – like I said, my one grandmother raised my father as a single woman in west Texas in a hotel, with one leg, and my other grandmother came from Kentucky in a covered wagon to the Indian Territories when she was twelve years old. I mean, really strong heavy-duty independent women!

"And so that image is in there too, and I remember writing 'standin' on the gone side of leaving' and it just tumbled out, I didn't really think about it. It was stream of consciousness, it was not conjured up, it was there. It's the writing that makes it my favourite song."

Sometimes playing live, he will switch the verses around: "I go back and forth. Sometimes I think, oh, this verse should go here, but it really doesn't matter. I do that with my songs all the time, change stuff around. They're mine. What snapped me into doing that, was I did it by accident one night, just not paying attention, just did the third verse second, and I went wow! that's great!"

Nanci Griffith recorded *She Ain't Goin' Nowhere* on her 1996 BLUE ROSES FROM THE MOONS album: "It's always been my favourite song of Guy's. It felt like it was my life story the first time I heard it. You know, Guy writes like Larry McMurtry, the novelist, he's extraordinary at writing a woman's feelings, finding that place in a woman's heart.

"I first met Guy and Susanna in, I guess it would have been 1976

On stage, Dallas, c.1975 (Ron McKeown)

at the Kerrville Music Festival, but I came across Guy initially through Townes Van Zandt and my father, because my father was a big fan, and also through Jerry Jeff Walker doing Guy's songs. I loved Guy's music, because it was like the music that I had grown up listening to, and the characters were so vivid and strong, and he was a Texas writer, and me being a Texas writer myself it was just a real big thing for me.

"I think that Townes Van Zandt was such a major influence on my early work, in my young teenage years, and then Guy came along, and they were both major influences. I kind of look at them as, you know, they're total opposites in writing: whereas Townes was more of an internalised writer – he wrote about matters of the heart, like Kate Wolf, very very good at internalising matters and bringing out his personal feelings – Guy is extraordinary at writing wonderful fiction, incredible stories and characters together. So they're very much opposites, but because they're of the same time and because they lived their lives as brothers, we all tend to lump them together."

The album opens with *Rita Ballou*, a joyous paeon to every 'rawhide rope and velvet mixture' barroom dancer who ever trod the boards of a Texas honky tonk:

She could dance that slow Uvalde
Shuffle to some cowboy hustle
How she made them trophy buckles
Shine shine shine

"Well actually it is fun," says Guy, "but that song, as opposed to *Coat From the Cold*, is kind of a tongue in cheek song, but it's laughing at yourself and lending some dignity to *her*. It's not like she's just a honky tonk floozy, she's the shit, she's the only person with dignity in that song, if you listen to it."

The final song on the album, *Let Him Roll*, marks the first time that Guy used a spoken format for one of his story songs, although other people have recorded different Guy Clark songs in the same way, notably Slim Pickens' version of *Desperados*. The guitar part is virtually identical to that Guy employed later in his other great spoken word song, *The Randall Knife*; here it provides a simple, beautiful background to the story of a old wino sitting on the roadside recalling the days of his youth, falling in love with a Dallas whore:

He could cut through the years to the very night
That it ended in a whorehouse fight
And she turned the last proposal down
In favor of bein' a girl about town

"It's funny," says Guy, "I wrote two songs that day. We were living in East Nashville and I was really pissed at Townes and Susanna, about something that they had said to me, and proceeded to take some tenpenny nails, a little hammer, my guitar and a bottle of wine and nailed myself into the bedroom! Fuck 'em! Leave me alone! And sat there and wrote these two songs. Wrote all of *Let Him Roll* and another funny talking song.

"Well, after some time I had to pee, and this old house we lived in had storm windows on it, you know, glass on the outside, and it was all painted shut, I couldn't get the window open to pee out the window. So I decided I was going to swallow my pride, pull the nails, well I had hammered these big tenpenny nails in this oak door and woodwork with a little bitty hammer – and it went in just fine. But I couldn't pull it out of that oak with that little fuckin' hammer. And I was trapped! And it was just like, what have I done? And I don't remember how I got out, some combination of Townes pushin' and me pullin'. Oh man.

"But anyway, it's about a character that Townes and I knew in Houston. His name was Sinbad, that's what everybody called him because he was an old merchant marine guy who lived in a little hotel, was the elevator man and hung out at this joint called the Old Quarter – have you ever heard the album LIVE AT THE OLD QUARTER, by Townes? – well, that's the place where I met him. So anyway, I took that character and wrote that story – the story is fiction, but the character is Sinbad."

Townes himself, in the 1977 Richard Wootton interview, comes across as feeling nostalgic for those days even after only four or five years had passed. And he mentions the nailing-in episode as well, as does Susanna later on…

"Guy had this house in Nashville next to Mickey Newbury and I used to stay there and Dennis, Richard Dobson, Rex Bell and Mickey White from Houston and David Olney who showed up from North Carolina. Four or five years ago there seemed to be more camaraderie between singer/songwriters, that group of people. There used to be two or three houses where everyone lived. I can remember drinking vodka and playing guitar all day long. Nobody had proper jobs. The whole crew would come over. You don't see that anymore, everybody's got their own place now.

"One time Dennis and some of them contracted with Mickey Newbury to landscape his garden, build some sort of Japanese fountain, or something. Mickey left town for a week and they got their money out front. They bought beer and got drunk, then the last two days they got real panicky and thought they ought to get something done. So they ordered two tons of gravel which was just dumped by the drive on Mickey's yard and it blocked the driveway. They looked at it, freaked out, took the rest of the money, went to town and got drunk again. They never came back again and Mickey returned to find his driveway under gravel. As Guy had kinda set them up, he phoned him and he couldn't believe it, and wouldn't talk to him for a month.

"It's been a long time since we all hung out together. I was living with Guy and Susanna in East Nashville cutting THE LATE GREAT and it was a little house, a real tense shotgun-type house. It was real hot, we were real broke, and we spent a lot of time just sitting about the house. It got so intense one day that Guy just nailed himself in his room to get away from everybody! He used big 16 pin nails and later had to climb out through the window because he couldn't get the door unnailed – he'd used about five nails. Finally we had to break the door down.

"During that same kind of time when we were broke, we decided we'd have to go to town and get some money from Mickey Newbury, and it was decided that I would phone Mickey. I was kind of humming and hawing, thinking of a way to ask for the money, and he said, 'By the way, Townes, I think you might have a cheque over at Acuff Rose.' 'Oh, really!' We raced over there and rushed to get it to the bank because it was Friday, and in the morning we were broke again. We had 500 dollars, but all we had to show for it was a 20 dollar violin. I don't know where it went – food and drink, I guess. We'd been broke for so long that when we got it we just went crazy."

Jerry Jeff Walker contributed the liner notes to OLD NO.1, a free form verse tribute to Guy which ends:

Anyway
This album's been a long time comin'
I, for one, have waited
Till ol' Sleepy-John, Guy said
"All right,
Would you write my liner notes?"
And I said
(Just like I knew what we were doin')
"Sure"
May your music set you free

Jerry Jeff told us, "Gary B. White knows him longer than I do, they were roommates together when I met him in Houston. Gary has known him a long time. Gary wrote *Long Long Time* for Linda Ronstadt, he lives out in Pasadena, California. He's a charming old grump who bitches and complains in a wonderful way. But Gary calls Guy 'Sleepy John', and it's kind of – Guy's real easygoing, and he's, I don't know, his father was a lawyer, maybe that's where the dignity comes from."

Jim McGuire & Jerry Jeff Walker Nashville, c.1976 (Guy & Susanna Clark collection)

Gary himself credits Bob Bruno with the original 'Sleepy John' tag, but says he "might have chuckled and kinda carried it on," and explains how he came to be on the album:

"I got a telephone call from Jerry Jeff, he was out at Guy's place in Mount Juliet, Tennessee. It was almost a log cabin he had on the lake, the place had no heat, I stayed there one time when there was snow on the ground and he had to chop wood all day to keep a fire, it was a little too rustic for my taste! In fact we were freezing our buns off, but Guy used to love it; ever the handyman, he'd be out there with his axe cutting up wood. Jerry Jeff was doing quite well at that time and he said, I want you and Annie – my wife – to come out and see us, and I said I can't just take off and come, and he says I already bought the ticket, pick it up at the airport and come here! Guy had just done some recording for the first album, and sent me a copy, and I thought it was pretty damn good, you know."

The list of players on the sleeve of OLD NO.1 reads like a Nashville Who's Who of sessioneers, although the process of recording, as would become not uncommon throughout Guy's career, was less than straightforward:

"The musicians on the album were just whatever the hotshit band was at the time. Actually, that first album is demos. The first guy that produced it, I just did not like what he did, or his approach, or him, and by the time it was through, I just said no, I mean, if you put this out I'll change my name! So we went back and I think we actually pilfered the demos – the two-inch tape of the demos of all the songs we had recorded for the album, and basically used that for the album. So that first album was done twice!"

Emmylou Harris, whose first Nashville album PIECES OF THE SKY had come out the previous year, was brought in, along with other friends of Guy, to add her harmonies to the mix, although she had actually met Guy before being introduced to his music:

"I met them through Rodney Crowell, they're great pals. I got a song of Rodney's [*Bluebird Wine*] onto my first album and I had him join the Hot Band. And then, I guess it was on one of my first trips to Nashville to play, along comes Guy and Susanna Clark into my life, and now I can't imagine what my life was like before them! They're my family, you know.

Guy & Emmylou Harris, Los Angeles, 1976 (Art Fein)

"But I really wasn't aware of Guy's music. *Desperados* was probably the first song of Guy's I heard. But quite soon after that Guy did his first album, and I was around for that, as part of the Guy Clark Chorus – everybody singing on every song!"

Rodney himself, with his youth and energy, played a part in the sound of the album, but typically plays down the importance of his contribution: "I think Guy and Neil Wilburn were sweet enough to let me be around, because certainly I had some talent and some energy and enthusiasm, even though it wasn't really formed quite yet. I'm really grateful to them because they let me take a shot, and I think if I contributed, it was my enthusiasm for Guy's work that was infectious – it maybe instilled confidence in Guy, the fact that I was so enthusiastic and supportive about his work.

"And it was really fun, because this was character time, the early days here, with people like Skinny Dennis Sanchez and Bronco Newcombe, Mickey White, Richard Dobson. I mean, these were goofball characters, and all kinds of high jinks went on, it was just a great time, you know. Nashville today is more corporate, and I think back then it was just a way of life, I don't see these kind of characters now.

"Guy in his own way is a character, he certainly wasn't as silly, he wasn't a circus performer like a lot of the stuff that went on, but a character in his own way. If you look at someone like Willie Nelson's career, Willie was on the road, and he was kind of the eye of the storm with his band, his entourage, just a cast of characters around that amused Willie no end. But the difference with Guy is, he was a little more stationary at that time."

Critical response to the album was overwhelmingly positive, both in America and abroad. John Tobler's comments in the May 1976 issue of the British rock magazine *ZigZag* were typical: 'This record is a positive gem... Guy Clark has an exceptional talent and has made a record to treasure.' The magazine's readers in fact gave Clark probably his first (and possibly his only?) experience of topping a music chart, with *LA Freeway* staying at number one in their top thirty for several issues.

ZIGZAG TOP THIRTY

LAST MONTH	THIS MONTH	ALBUM TRACK (or single*)	ARTISTE
1	1	L.A. Freeway	GUY CLARK
-	2	Desperados Under The Eaves	WARREN ZEVON
2	3	Memory Motel	ROLLING STONES
8	4	Shake Some Action	FLAMIN GROOVIES
3	5	Only Sixteen	DR HOOK
4	6	Cypress Avenue	VAN MORRISON

'A record to treasure' – Guy Clark at No.1!

The album also made an impression on some of the mainstream Nashville artists, like Johnny Cash, who covered three songs from it – *Texas–1947, Desperados* and *Let Him Roll* – over the next few years.

Texas Cookin'

THE next album, TEXAS COOKIN', followed a year later in 1976. Though not as immediately impressive as the first album, the tracks were strong and it included the first published song that Guy and Susanna had written together, *Black Haired Boy*:

"Susanna and I wrote that in Long Beach about the same time I wrote *Old Time Feeling*. We finished writing it and she said, who are you writing that about? I said, I was writing it about Townes, and she said, I was writing it about you! Well, people couldn't separate the three of us. With a crowbar! Yeah, we were three of a kind. Anyway, I like that song, and I don't do it near enough."

The title track was on a theme that crops up now and again in Guy Clark songs. There have always been songs written about food, from *Jambalaya* to *Boiled Beef and Carrots* – after all, as well as being essential to life, it's also one of its great sensual pleasures:

"Well, *Texas Cookin'* is what it is, being in Tennessee and not having any barbecue or Mexican food, you know, and also, I was trying to learn to play a Mance Lipscomb song, that style he plays, that Texas country blues guitar, and I had the lick before the song, I had the music. Also, it's one chord, it never changes chords, and to be able to pull that off was a pretty cool hot lick, you know. Because it's how you play it, the dynamics of it, that makes it work. But anyway, that song is just a laundry list of food, you know, and fun. And genuine, because I really did miss it! I wasn't just making it up."

The album contains two of Guy's most touching love songs. *Good To Love You Lady* echoes, less jokily, the homesickness of *Texas Cookin'*. The feeling that two people share, stranded in a foreign land, is ameliorated by the simple fact of them being there with each other. It's Texas and Tennessee in the song, but it could be Ireland and Australia. It's Guy and Susanna, but it could be any of us.

Here comes Texas rollin' through my mind
There ain't nothin' to it mama, don't be cryin'
It's just one of those things that everyone goes through
And everybody's got 'em some kind of past
Now here comes that old snake in the grass now
Lord it's good to be in Tennessee with you

You can feel Susanna's presence in every line of the other great love song on the album, *Anyhow I Love You*. Times aren't always easy

Guy in Grelun Landon's office, RCA Records, Hollywood 1976 (Art Fein)

in any relationship, and sometimes you just have to remind each other of the basics:

I wish I had a dime for every bad time
But the bad times always seem to keep the change
You've been all alone, so you know what I'm saying
And when all you can recall is the pain,

Just you wait until tomorrow when you wake up with me
by your side and find I haven't lied about nothin'
And I wouldn't trade a tree for the way I feel
about you in the mornin' anyhow I love you

"*Anyhow I Love You* is pretty cool. I always thought that was just kind of a goofy song, but I get a request for that every time I play, every time. Even though it's got that chorus which I thought wouldn't make sense to anyone: 'I wouldn't trade a tree for the way I feel about you'. And people like that. It's not that I don't think it's good, I thought it was just a little too off the wall for people to really – for it to be a serious song. Or something, I don't know. Once again, I still do it."

The album winds up with two 'ballads', although the first is actually a little jaunt along the Texas coast in a shrimper: "*The Ballad of Laverne and Captain Flint* is another one of those wrong titles. The name of that song is 'Old Flint's Boat'. I mean, that's one of the last times I titled a song! I just never changed that one."

The other, which reads almost like John Wayne's final film THE SHOOTIST from another angle, is *The Last Gunfighter Ballad,* an echo of the old west brought up to date.

"That is one of my favourite pieces of writing. When I was about 8 or 9, the guy that taught me to play dominoes was about eighty and he had been in the last real horse cavalry in the south west. When he was a kid he hung out in Belle Starr's saloon – she was a famous outlaw in New Mexico – and all of a sudden it snapped to me that, you take a kid, 17, 18 years old, wants to be a gunfighter in 1885 and lives to be 80, that puts him smack dab in the middle of the twentieth century. And those kind of time spans always fascinated me.

"And the twist was him getting killed by a car! A little off the wall. But that's the subject. The way I envisioned that song being sung was in an Irish pub, with everybody singing on the chorus, you know – 'Curse the smell of the black powder smoke…' – it's like a wake song, almost."

Talking to Richard Wootton in 1982, Clark remarked how the era has been romanticised in films and books: "Of course it didn't happen like that. There wasn't really a 'Code of the West' and people standing off in the streets – I mean you'd shoot a guy in the back if you could get away with it! The whole of the 'Gunfight at the OK Corral' all took place within about five feet. Shotguns at about five feet! They just happened around a corner and ran into each other. It certainly wasn't choreographed."

The musicians on the album, which was again produced by Neil Wilburn but mostly recorded at Chips Moman's American Studios in Nashville, were largely the same as on OLD NO. 1, but various others – Chris Laird on drums and Charlie Bundy on bass – were brought in to the sessions, together with guitarists Danny Rowland and Brian Ahern. Photographer Jim McGuire, who has been a friend of Guy and Susanna for many years and has worked on the covers of all his albums, took a playful shot of various members of the TEXAS COOKIN' sessions around this time. McGuire explains:

"The one with the pyramid? Yeah, we used to have parties at my studio, pickin' parties, drinkin' parties, whatever parties, and it came out of one of those. The guy that's looking through the girl's legs is Danny Rowland; the one on the right side with a moustache, kind of a thin guy, his name's Chris Laird, he was the drummer in one of Guy's early bands. The guy in the middle on the bottom is Mickey Raphael, Willie Nelson's harmonica player, and that's his girlfriend on top. The guy on the floor is Curt Allen, I think he was just a friend of Guy's, I don't think he actually played in the band, and on top of Guy with the Willie Nelson t-shirt is Charlie Bundy.

"I don't remember the very first time I met Guy but it was probably through Michael Brovsky, his manager at the time, I knew Brovsky through Jerry Jeff. Guy and I both came to town the same year, around 72, but the first time I really hung out was for the photo session for the OLD NO. 1 album, Michael Brovsky set me up to shoot

Guy (bottom right) and Susanna (middle left) Nashville, 1976 – see text for others (Jim McGuire)

that job. Actually I hadn't heard his music at that time. When I did, I thought it was brilliant, I'd never really heard anything like it. We became fast friends, he used to come by the studio all the time, I had a little storefront studio over in west Nashville and at that time I was playing dobro and so we used to have these kinda impromptu pickin' sessions, he'd call people and I would call people, probably once a week or so, Rodney and Steve Earle and all those people he was hanging out with at the time, it was pretty amazing. I played with Guy a few times locally. I never felt I was really good enough to sit in with him but he talked me into it a couple of times when he played showcases or shows here in town I did actually sit in with him, playing dobro. And we used to go to his house too, to parties, just sit around and play in the living room.

"I quickly connected with him, because he's a visual artist as well and he had spent time in Houston; one of the jobs he had there was an art director of a TV station. He was pretty much into the visual side of it, he was painting some, and we became friends because I was also playing music for fun, so we had mutual interests."

We asked Jim whether Guy was a difficult subject to work with, given his own visual art interest:

"Not at all. Guy was always real kinda comfortable being photographed, he was one of those people who didn't care about what happened in front of the camera, he was really just himself, which was really easy in a lot of ways. He was easy to photograph – it didn't matter if the camera was on him or not, he would sort of just be himself. A lot of people aren't like that, they really change when the camera's on them. That's what was so great, that's why I've got so much great film.

"Except when he's on the road I probably see him every week. We've been great friends the whole time. We go out together a lot, and to the house a lot, and he comes to the studio. Guy helped in the way of introducing me to people, especially Texas people that I didn't know or wasn't familiar with – Joe Ely and those kind of people that I hadn't heard up until then; he's actually a huge fan of what I do so he spreads the word, gives me a good plug whenever he can."

On the later album covers, Jim is often credited as 'Señor McGuire': "There was a time a few years ago when I spent a lot of time in Mexico. I used to go down there and work for two, three months, shooting commercial stuff like hotel brochures and that kind of thing, just to get out of Nashville, and going to meetings down there with the Mexicans, that's how I was introduced, Señor McGuire! So it was just like a nickname that everybody started using and sorta stuck, a lot of people still call me that!"

Around this time – although due to financial and distribution problems it wasn't fully released even in America until years later – a film was produced which featured, among other artists, the music of Guy, Townes and Rodney. The film was HEARTWORN HIGHWAYS, (sometimes called 'New Country') made by the young director James Szalapski. Unhurried and heavy on atmosphere, the film suffers from spreading its net too widely; whilst a lot of the music is wonderful, and some of the non-musical segments (particularly Townes showing the camera crew round his dilapidated smallholding) are worth watching, you have to put up with (or fast forward through) interminable pieces featuring David Allan Coe, Charlie Daniels and others. But there is an almost unbearably poignant sequence early on where Townes and Susanna are sitting with an old blacksmith, Seymour Washington, who quietly weeps as Townes sings *Waitin' Round to Die*. Later in the film Rodney plays a nicely raw *Bluebird Wine*.

Guy himself is seen playing two complete songs: an outdoor performance of *That Old Time Feeling*, accompanied by Steve Young on slide guitar, and *Texas Cookin'*, filmed in the studio. In 1981 Jan Hoffman wrote in the New York *Village Voice*: 'Guy Clark, black eyebrows clenched as he sings, is easily the most interesting musician, and the film's quiet good guy.' Hoffman also describes the end of the film, with many of the principals, including a youthful Steve Earle, sitting around a long sturdy wooden table: 'Christmas Eve at Guy's place: a late night clutter of ashtrays, empty bourbon bottles, wine glasses, flickering lamps, musical instruments, kids, men and women all singing. *Silent Night,* country style – a dobro moan promises respite from loneliness.' Pauline Kael in the *New Yorker* emphasised the director's rapport with the performers: 'He understands that we're interested not only in Guy Clark's beautiful, mournful voice but also in his dignified manner and his humility (he's like a Quaker pacifist) and in how they relate to his music.'

In 1978 Guy talked to Allan Jones about the film, and Townes' contribution in particular:

"He was the best thing in that movie. If you think about it, Townes is the only guy in that whole movie who didn't try to play it like the camera wasn't there. The minute that camera started runnin', he just turned to face it, straight on an' said, 'Hi, I'm Townes Van Zandt!' He's just the most extraordinary character. The best as far as I'm concerned. Can't think of anyone who comes close.

"Sure, he can be self-destructive. And he knows it. He was just in a pretty bad accident. He was riding in a truck with another guy and they ran into a tree. He broke his arm and a couple of ribs. Had 30 stitches in his face. But, hell he lives out the lifestyles he chooses to live. It's his own choice. He's smart, though; as smart as anyone I know. But it's his life, he makes his own choices. He lives his life the way he wants to. I guess that's as much as anyone can do."

We get the opportunity in the film to catch a glimpse of Guy the

Guy with Travis Clark, c.1977 (Jim McGuire)

craftsman: refretting and fitting a new bridge to a guitar and explaining to the owner why he's using particular methods and materials. One of the more intimate moments is when Guy is tuning the newly-repaired guitar, and helping him is a small boy, a very young Travis Clark, who recalls:

"Oh yes, I remember it very well, I was about 8 or 10. That was shot in Mount Juliet, east of Nashville, at the house that Guy lived in, the house that Townes passed away in, matter of fact."

Guy, Rodney, Emmylou & John Hartford on stage at McCabe's, Los Angeles, 1976 (Art Fein)

The Warner Years

Guy Clark was very much part of the Nashville scene by this time, and his songs were being recorded by established country artists – Jerry Jeff Walker and Johnny Cash in particular – but his records certainly hadn't caught fire commercially. A third album was started in 1977, but as so often during his career, Guy's ideas and those of his current record company – in this case, RCA – were not exactly compatible.

In his 1978 interview with Allan Jones, just after he left RCA, Clark was forthright about the company:

"We had all kinds of problems with them, problems with the budgets for the albums; havin' the amount of money it takes to do it right, you know. They didn't know what to do with me. They didn't know how to market the records. They knew they were good, but they didn't know what to do with them. And they couldn't understand why I couldn't just go into the studio with six Nashville session guys and just do it… you know, a nice, comfortable country album. But I held out for people who would be involved, who'd commit themselves musically to those albums. RCA were just too busy selling Elvis Presley records and making a star out of John Denver, I guess."

His attitude seems to have mellowed by 1982, when he told Richard

Wootton how he went to an RCA executive and asked to be released from his contract, which still required him to produce some more albums:

"I explained to him, 'It's just not happening right and I'm not getting the kind of support and understanding I need,' and he just gave me back the contract, which was a very nice thing for him to do. Then we were free to hop around the market place, and Warner Brothers were very interested."

Emmylou Harris had been with Warner Brothers from the start of her career (excepting her 1970 solo album GLIDING BIRD on Jubilee); Rodney Crowell had just signed with them and was about to release his first album. Guy and Susanna had been close to Rodney and Emmylou since they had arrived in Nashville, and while they were hanging out with them, Guy met Andy Wickham, an Englishman who ran Warner's country division. Wickham liked what Guy was doing and wanted him to come over, and Guy eventually signed.

This led to the first opportunity we in England had to see Guy. Emmylou had done some very successful raids on London in the previous three years, bringing the Hot Band over to play at the New Victoria and Hammersmith Odeon theatres, as well as the Royal Albert Hall, at first with James Burton on lead guitar and later with Albert Lee. In September 1978 Warner Brothers decided to make the most of their three major 'new country' acts, and brought them over as the Warner Country show, touring several major European cities. For two nights in London the venue was again the Hammersmith Odeon. The Guy Clark Band was to open the show, followed by Rodney Crowell, with Emmylou and the Hot Band closing.

The shows were an unalloyed success, particularly for Guy. Don Ford wrote in *Country Music Roundup*: 'It was a night of brilliance… from the moment that Guy Clark strode on stage, the smoke from his cigarette stuck on his guitar curling away into the stage lighting, he gave a superlative performance.'

Colin Irwin in *Melody Maker* also pointed out the short-sightedness of his record label: 'Had RCA had the elementary intelligence to bring Clark to Britain a couple of years ago, continuing the momentum of his albums OLD NO.1 and TEXAS COOKIN', then he'd surely be topping Hammersmith Odeon for three nights in his own right. His hour-

Guy & Susanna, Nashville, 1978
(Guy & Susanna Clark collection)

long set was, with embarrassing ease, the best of the night.'

John Tobler was one of Guy's long-time cheerleaders in Britain, and gushed about the gig in the first issue of the short-lived magazine *Up Country*: 'Hell, I didn't expect anything remotely as good as this! It's rare to experience such a magical performance. If you've got the records already, and can imagine them done the right side of perfect, that's what we heard. If you haven't got the records, don't read this, just go and get them, OK? Make no mistake, this was one of the most mercurial and brilliant performances I've seen in years, and if Guy Clark doesn't get back over here fast, I'll write to my MP.'

Even Guy himself said he "thoroughly enjoyed the experience", although talking with Allan Jones after the first night, his feelings about the size of the venues he was being booked into were already becoming apparent: "Halls that size are as big as I like to play. We played some *real* big places once when we went out with Waylon…

we did rodeo arenas and football fields. There'd be like 10-15,000 people and it got outta hand. It's just not comfortable as far as bein' able to communicate is concerned. I like to think people can actually hear what I'm playin'. I don't play rowdy dance music. I'd rather play a club, you know, than try to take on a rowdy honky tonk where the audience would just sooner dance and drink beer. So when it comes to one of those real big joints, I'd say, 'gimme a saloon, any day'."

The band was as good in its own way as Emmylou's, with Freddy Joe Fletcher on drums, Bea Spears (from Willie Nelson's band) on bass, Rodney Crowell's cousin Larry Willoughby on rhythm and Dave Perkins on lead guitar, with Lea Jane Berinati, who had appeared on the RCA records, playing keyboards. Most of the set was naturally taken from the first two albums, but there were two numbers we hadn't heard before, *Fools For Each Other* and the Jimmie Rodgers song *In the Jailhouse Now*, both of which were to turn up on the new album. Guy took full advantage of the occasion, responding to the crowd and encoring with *The Last Gunfighter Ballad*.

Unfortunately, according to Phil Kaufman, then and now Emmylou's road manager, he didn't realise the state of the London Underground railway at the time – the trains tended to stop running before 11 o'clock. Kaufman remembers how hard it was to get him and the band to finish their set: "We were doing this show at the Hammersmith Odeon with Emmylou and the Hot Band, and Guy was opening the show, and we couldn't get him off stage, he didn't realise that the longer he stayed on, the less Emmylou could play because of the curfew, the trains shut down, so I just went to the side of the stage and yelled *Get 'em off!* He thought I meant sexually! I couldn't get his attention, he just kept going on and on!"

His first album for Warner, titled simply GUY CLARK, came out later in 1978. There was continuity on the production side from the two RCA albums – it was again produced by Neil Wilburn for Free Flow, and the players were much the same as on TEXAS COOKIN' – but musically it was a strange mixture of his own material, some of which was totally unlike anything we had heard from him before, and versions of other people's songs.

The choice of the covers was eclectic and quite strong: Rodney

Crowell's *Voila, An American Dream,* which had just appeared on his own solo album; Walter Martin Cowart's *One Paper Kid; In the Jailhouse Now;* and Townes Van Zandt's *Don't You Take it Too Bad,* the first song by Townes that Guy had recorded:

"Yeah, that's one of the first songs Townes ever wrote, or the first I heard him sing – I still do it almost every night – and talk about seamless… no chorus, just a great song."

The album opens with *Fool On the Roof,* a strange, funky number with obscure lyrics (about the devil in your head?), and closes with the obviously, if not musically, related *Fool On the Roof Blues,* a weird, sparsely instrumented (just bass, guitar and harmonica) irregular blues with, perhaps revealingly, the final words on the whole album: 'I'm talkin' about goin' back to Texas – just me, my guitar and my wife.'

The standout on the album is another love song, *Fools For Each Other,* which Guy played on the tour and still does live. A slowish ballad with a nice acoustic guitar break by Rodney – and even the string section doesn't detract from the song as much as on some of the other numbers – it simply lists the reasons two lovers have stayed together through thick and thin:

Now who gave up when the fire burned low
Who flew south when the wind blew cold
It wasn't me, it wasn't you
Who held on when the blues came down
Who took care when the tie was bound
That was you, darlin', and that was me

In spite of the success of his first live shows in Europe, there was a general feeling when the GUY CLARK album came out that perhaps this was the end of the Guy Clark records we had come to love over the last few years – that somehow he was being pushed towards a more rock-orientated audience in order to gain commercial respectability. Even the cover pictures, moody poses showing him with a beard, made a depressing change from the joyful photos of Guy and Susanna on the RCA albums. The album was the last one of his to be manufactured and distributed locally: nowadays, with the changing multinational structure of the industry and the complete replacement of vinyl LPs with CDs, this is not such a big deal, but at that time the difficulties of importing records meant that British fans did not get to hear of any new American releases until much later.

This was unfortunate, since the next album, released in 1980 and the first to be produced by Rodney Crowell, brought a return to form that gave us unexpected gems like the title track, *South Coast of Texas*, a glorious celebration of life on the Gulf Coast margins:

The south coast of Texas, that's a thin slice of life
It's salty and hard, it is stern as a knife
Where the wind is for blowin' up hurricanes for showin'
Snakes how to swim and trees how to lean

"That's a song I do all the time. The original idea of the song, what I was thinking about when I had the idea of trying to write it was, on the south coast of Texas there are all of these different languages you hear spoken, because the waters of the world are an international place – it doesn't matter whether you are Vietnamese or Texan, or Cajun, or Mexican, or what, you can make a living by the sea, by shrimping, or catching fish. And that is a universal language. And I was trying to get up the flavour of that by singing 'adios jole blon' which is Mexican and French. A feeble attempt maybe, but anyway, that's what that song was about.

"Plus I got to use Gilbert Roland in it – and the dignity of whooping cranes, of which there were only 26 in the world at that time. Gilbert Roland's an American movie actor, always had the little pencil-thin moustache, real swarthy Greek or Spanish looking with big leather wristbands, played in all the adventure movies. You got to have Gilbert Roland to make a living by the sea! Very few people get that, a lot of times people go who the hell's Gilbert Roland? Well, let me tell you...! I've got a studio publicity picture of him someone gave me. Ran across it when we were looking through those pictures the other day, I didn't think about it. Next time you see him you'll recognise him. I think he played Zorro. Or the Cisco Kid."

There's altogether a more open, optimistic tone to the album, even to the inclusion of an oddity in *Heartbroke*, one of the most upbeat heartbreak songs you'll ever hear. Not one of Guy's personal favourites, it was nevertheless covered by Rodney Crowell on his 1980 album BUT WHAT WILL THE NEIGHBOURS THINK, and subsequently provided Clark's biggest hit as a writer when Ricky Skaggs, who played on the original track, took a pop/bluegrass version to the top of the country charts in 1982.

Another odd choice was a remake of *Rita Ballou*, from the first album: "Somebody talked me into it, this hotshit band we had, the Mudflaps! I mean, it was a really good studio band. They thought it would be a commercial song to do it in a more rock'n'roll approach as opposed to the more folky fingerstyle that it was on the first record. The opportunity was presenting itself to get that played on the radio – with the urging of my manager and the record company both – and so I did. Once again, no sell-out too small... And they're both pretty cool versions, you know, I like them both."

There are several other songs on the album that tell of struggle against adversity of one kind or another. *Crystelle* is the story of another woman, again taken from life once removed:

"It's based on a character, a woman who was my grandmother's friend when I was a little bitty kid. She had flaming red hair, not a floozy, but she was a hairdresser in west Texas, she had a beer joint. She was not quite as old as my grandmother but died before my grandmother, but when she was young she must have been a knockout, you know, and I just kind of based this character on her. I haven't actually played it in about ten years. Every once in a while I think about relearning it.

"*New Cut Road* is the story I was telling you about my grandmother who was born in Kentucky – her older brother's name was Coleman Bonner, and he was a fiddle player. And I just kind of loosely based it around what I remember of the stories hearing as a kid, about the family. The song I was trying to write, always wanted to, maybe still will, is about my grandmother, about the time when she went from Kentucky to the Indian Territory and Texas in a covered wagon, when she was twelve years old in 1894. And before she died she saw men walk on the moon, live and in colour on TV. So those kind of songs that twist always fascinate me.

"I really like *The Partner Nobody Chose*. Rodney and I did it the other night in Austin. It's just this pretty little song, we call it our Carter Family song, because it's such a beautiful traditional old melody." Rodney, who co-wrote it, agrees about the Carter Family reference:

"Yeah, I think so, it just has that kind of innocence – the thing about Carter Family music at its best, you know, *Wildwood Flower*, all those things, they're very innocent, and the language is really kind of old fashioned language, and I think that's what that song is like – definitely a folk song."

The second Clark/Crowell song on the album is *She's Crazy For Leaving*, for which Rodney seems almost embarrassed at having a writing credit: "Actually, both those songs were ideas that Guy had in development, and when we started to get together to do the pre-production he said, I got these songs, what do I do with these, and I just helped him finish them, you know, basically he did most of the

Rodney and Guy going through 'No Deal'
during the 'Better Days' sessions, 1983 (Jim McGuire)

work on those songs. I helped him more on *The Partner Nobody Chose*, but *She's Crazy For Leaving*, that was pretty much intact – I got a freebie on that one!"

Another two years passed before the next album, BETTER DAYS, in 1983. The third and last of the Warner Brothers records, it was again produced by Rodney Crowell, using mostly the same musicians – almost an extended Hot Band – as on the previous album, although this time in Nashville. The front cover shows a very spruced-up Guy Clark in dress shirt and jacket, with his guitar on his knee and a bluebird on his shoulder. Everything is satisfactual!

Rodney, however, is certainly not as happy with his contribution to BETTER DAYS as he was with the previous album, which, being his first production credit, has a more spontaneous feel:

"The first record we made together was SOUTH COAST OF TEXAS. Guy had already made a record, but said he wasn't happy with it. He had a little money left over in his recording budget, so we got together and said, let's go into the recording studio and we'll do it really quick, we'll fix you up! So we made that record in about two weeks, and the stuff worked, and it was fun, it really went well. But with the second record, BETTER DAYS, Guy had some really good songs, and personally I think that my work – you know, I was getting a little more into being a professional producer by then – was a little spotty. I mean some of his songs on that record were really excellent, and I didn't do the job of bringing them to life, you know."

Two boat songs are included on the album. *Blowin' Like a Bandit*, with some 'so bad they're good' rhymes, gives dire warnings to shrimpers about storms out on the ocean; and *Supply and Demand* is another scene from a story based on fact, as Clark explains:

"That song kind of got away from me, but I intend to start doing it again. I just saw the guy I wrote that about down in Florida. He's a real guy who's a stone crab fisherman, and years ago some guys he knew paid him a whole lot of money to just store some bales of marijuana overnight. And he wasn't involved in the deal, all he did was say, you can put them in my barn. And got busted. And didn't turn the other guys in. And did like, I don't know, some long time in jail. Very noble cat!"

The record contained two of Guy's little gems. *Tears* is a gentle western swing tune ('Whoever said the hand is quicker than the eye has never tried to brush away a tear') in the vein of Bob Wills' *San Antonio Rose*, and in *Better Days*, a woman is getting her life back together after some unstated trauma:

Standing at the window, her face to the glass
As far as she can see the time has come to pass
As far as she can see the sky is all ablaze
And this looks like the first of better days

Along with *Homegrown Tomatoes* and *The Carpenter*, it's a song from the album that Guy still does in concerts:

"That's just a song, very similar to *She Ain't Going Nowhere*, a little vignette, a little snapshot. I was down in Australia playing and somebody asked for that tune, and I said, I don't really do it any more because there was a verse in there, or a couple of lines I didn't really like, and this woman who asked me about it worked in a shelter for battered women. She said it was kind of their theme song, and she asked me what the lines were, and I told her, and I said I thought they were kinda bullshit, you know, and she said, yeah, all the battered women think that too! So I sat down and figured it out that night, and I've been doing it ever since.

"*Homegrown Tomatoes*, now, is a love song. I had a garden, was watching my tomato plants grow, just like, wow, look at that! Those little guys need a love song. So I wrote one – it's not a novelty song!" It is in fact one of the few songs recorded by Guy Clark that ever received substantial radio airplay on the country stations, the others being *Fools For Each Other* and *The Partner Nobody Chose*.

But aside from *The Randall Knife*, which we'll come to next in the book, the album's masterpiece – and one of the defining songs of Guy Clark's entire output – is *The Carpenter*. Guy sometimes says at his gigs, when he plays Townes' song *To Live is to Fly*, that it's "words to live by", and that is just how many people think of the lyrics of *The Carpenter*:

He was tough as a crowbar, quick as a chisel
Fair as a plane and true as a level

In the studio, 'Better Days' sessions, 1983
(l-r) Vince Gill, Rodney, Emory Gordy, Guy, Hank de Vito (Jim McGuire)

He was straight as a chalk line and right as a rule
Square with the world, he took good care of his tools

The Randall Knife is in some ways Guy Clark's most personal song. In it, he talks candidly about the relationship between a father and his son and the personal connection that an inanimate object revered by both can somehow strengthen, the quality of the Randall knife ('if a better blade was ever made it was probably forged in Hell') being used as a metaphor for the quality of the relationship.

Guy Clark's music is peopled with characters whose lives and emotions can be shared and understood, and in that sense many of the songs can seem to act as 'Randall Knives' themselves, facilitating our own connections to the parts of our experience that it is sometimes hard to access.

Both of Clark's released recordings of the song use the rolling guitar accompaniment first heard in a slightly different form on *Let Him Roll*, but the first version on BETTER DAYS is far more rhythmic than Guy's own preference: the sparse, almost ad lib reading on the much later DUBLIN BLUES.

Interlude: THE RANDALL KNIFE

GUY Clark's den, downstairs in his west Nashville home, has a workbench along one side, with his guitar-making and repairing tools arrayed neatly on the wall above it. On the opposite wall is stacked hundreds of cassette tapes: recordings made at gigs, demos, tapes of Townes' songs and Susanna's; and in front some recording equipment, which is covered over with a sheet when any work is being done at the bench.

In the middle of the room is a long wooden table. We sat with Guy around this table for two afternoons, talking about his life, his songs, his friends. He showed us the early stages of the classical guitars he is making with Verlon Thompson, and he brought out black and white photographs, taken over many years, of Guy himself and the people in his life.

Sometime during one of the sessions, we'd been discussing the *South Coast of Texas* song and Gilbert Roland, and for a while were just small-talking.

"Are you a big movie fan?" asked Nick.

"Some movies," said Guy in his slow, warm Texas drawl. "I watch TV movies, I don't go to movies. It's just getting to be too much of a hassle to get up and go to a theatre and stand in line, and pay ten bucks and not be able to smoke a cigarette or have a drink, just sit there and watch."

"What sort of movies would you watch?"

"Watch all kinds of stuff, you know, I like different things. Older movies are my favourite, you know, *Yojimbo*, the Kurasawa movie; *La Strada*, Fellini's first movie with Anthony Quinn and Giulietta Masina; *A Boy and His Dog*, kind of a science fiction story by a writer named Harlan Ellison."

"You're an artist yourself," said Jeff, "does that influence your songwriting?"

"I paint, yes. I think because painting is more of a hand/eye co-ordination thing, whereas writing is more cerebral – the right- and left-brain thing – I find that they complement one another, as does working with wood, or throwing darts. I've sat with two tables set up and built a model airplane and wrote at the same time, just to get the other side of the brain going. The minute you start doing one, something will occur to you about the other. In this particular setup I don't really have a place to paint and write at the same time, it's not big enough to have a painting snug big enough to do that. Actually I have a couple of paintings, they're usually hanging here…"

Guy went in to the office next door and brought in a self-portrait, the powerful original cover painting for the OLD FRIENDS album, and one of Rodney, and a picture of a very tall, thin man with a moustache, a hat and a drink in one hand. Jeff said, "Is this Skinny Dennis?"

"Yes, but it's not a very good painting. His name was Dennis Sanchez. But he's dead, he's been dead for years. He was like six-eight, weighed 135 pounds. He had a disease that was actually the same one that Abraham Lincoln had, elongation of the limbs, and what it does, it means your heart has to pump blood further, and consequently you have a very weak heart, and you have to take very good care of yourself. Which Dennis did not do! And would not do. Even though he knew. Actually he died one night on stage playing bass, years ago."

We looked at the painting for a while, then Guy showed us the photograph it was taken from *(see p.35)*. He put another photo on the table. "That's my favourite picture of Susanna – fairly pissed with me and Townes one time we were drunk round at someone's house!"

"How did you meet Susanna?" Nick asked.

Susanna with Townes (under poncho) and Geraldine (Guy & Susanna Clark collection)

"I met her in Oklahoma. I was a friend of her sister, and they lived in Oklahoma City. I was up there playing music, Townes and I. Been married some 26 years. A long time."

"Two artists together – does that work?"

Guy laughed. "So far!" He pulled out another photo. "This is Susanna and Townes – somebody made Townes a poncho that says 'and Lefty' – and the dog Geraldine. And this is when we first moved to Nashville – that was about the time *LA Freeway* was written, the time I nailed myself into the bedroom, that was the house it happened in. That other guy's Daniel, crazy hippie friend of Townes that he told that story about – the intro to *Pancho and Lefty*, you heard that?"

"I've often wondered why Townes isn't on any of your albums," said Jeff.

"I don't think I'm on any of his either! Oh, I don't know, Townes and I, that wasn't part of the deal, you know, it's like that wasn't – and we both knew neither one of us could sing or play good enough to be of any help other than a quote personality, and both of us kind of abhorred that, you know, so we avoided it or whatever, I don't know. I think it's a shame, I have a ton of tape – Townes and I used to go out at a certain point as a duo, you know, booked together, both headliners, and we went on stage together from the very beginning of the set and just talked and traded songs and told stories for a couple of hours. But as far as trying to sing or play with one another, it was pretty gruesome! We had the odd moment… but I have a lot of tape of that. Good quality tape."

Nick said, "You're spoken about like brothers by a lot of people, there's a great deal of respect there."

"Well, as it should be. I mean, we were as close as you could get, closer than brothers, you know. It's hard to describe."

The room went quiet for a moment. Nick said, "Is this okay to talk about Townes?"

"Oh, sure, man, I love talking about Townes."

"Did he help in a practical sense with the songwriting?"

Townes, Susanna, Guy and Daniel, Nashville, c.1972
(Guy & Susanna Clark collection)

"Oh no, just through what he was doing inspired me to write. No, I never wrote with Townes, we rarely discussed songwriting – if you had to talk about it, it wasn't the same, you know what I mean? It's like, it was beyond a nuts and bolts discussion, you either did it or you didn't. And the inspiration was not to be like Townes but to able to find that place within yourself to write, not like Townes but like you. I have no idea how I found that place, I'm still confused! One of the reasons I like *Dublin Blues* so much is because it's more like a Townes song, plus it's the only song of mine that Townes ever recorded. Except for *Don't Let the Sunshine Fool You*, which doesn't count."

"Why doesn't that count?"

"Oh, because it's not a very good song, I don't think. Matter of fact, that's a song I wrote before *Old Time Feeling*. It was an old song I wrote which I thought was just..."

The thought trailed away into silence. Guy sipped his drink.

"Do you know when you're going to write a song?" asked Nick.

"Well, there's a certain amount of discipline to it that I try to enforce upon myself, but I don't know when it's going to happen – other than, well, I've gotta get some songs written, tomorrow I'm gonna start, OK, it's gonna happen! – but as far as those little flashes of inspiration, I try and write them down when they happen. Because you will forget them – in the middle of the night, or five minutes later – so the only real discipline I employ is to, when I think of a little idea, I write it down on a napkin, or a piece of paper or whatever."

"You said *Old Time Feeling* was the first song you kept. Presumably you'd written a lot before, and threw them away..."

"I didn't throw them away! I don't throw away anything – I have them all. Doesn't make any sense to throw it away – you might be able to go back and steal something from yourself!"

"Your songs all have good tunes, strong tunes in themselves."

"Which is hard to do when I have my range to work with! It's pretty tricky!"

"I can connect with that," said Nick, "your range is the same as mine."

"Early on," Guy continued, "I learned, probably from that kind of thing, that less is more, it really is.There's a real Japanese negative space in painting, you know, and with great guitar players it ain't what they play, it's the holes they leave."

Nick felt a strong itching in his fingers, wanting to get a guitar out and demonstrate the point. He said, "When I play *Dublin Blues*, for example, it's all about the spaces – it almost hangs together with the holes."

"Of course, it does, it's meant to. I know what I'm doing! I do it on purpose – I have real trouble trying to perform songs that have the same beat all the way through. I mean, it's like, wait a minute, you know..."

"The gaps require you to listen, it's one of the ways you pull people in."

"It's Yin and Yang – it wouldn't be loud if it wasn't quiet, you wouldn't know the difference if it were all one level."

"Are you aware of pulling the audience along?"

"Of course I am, I mean, I know when it's good and when it's not – sometimes I can't get into it or I can't hear – loud drunks or whatever – and I just turn off and kinda do it by rote. But I know when it's really good too."

These words triggered off a recent memory for Nick. He said, "We saw Robert Earl Keen last night at Vanderbilt University."

"Did he have his band?"

"Yeah, and they were going crazy – that wouldn't happen at your kind of gig!"

"No, no, I hope not!"

"But it's a different kind of experience."

"I've talked to Robert about that. We used to go out and play a lot, him and Townes and I – he was getting that even then, just by himself."

"We were talking in the hotel after the gig, and he was saying there are certain songs he just can't do now, simply because he can't hear them."

"Right, right. Which to me is like a travesty, I mean, I refuse to let that happen. And it's very seductive because a kind of funny upbeat song will get you the big response. Especially if you keep doing one after another, and then you can't do – *Old Time Feeling* or *Desperados*, or *The Randall Knife*, you can't do it. So if you pace it right, do one, maybe two kinda jumpy songs, and then do something just so far down, you know."

Nick was thinking about the times he'd seen Guy performing in England. "You can play Wembley, or a folk club in Banbury, and you're going to pull people in if there's 50,000 or 50. What does it feel like, when you've got an audience, when you're happy, the sound's good, you're connected up –"

"It's what I do. *That's* what I *do*. Everything – the travel, anything else I do, tuning up, the sound check – is all attendant to that. And that's what I do. When that works – wow, I was right! You know what I mean! And if it's a bummer, it's a bummer, and that's just part of it, it's not going to be right every night. You wouldn't know it was fun unless it was shit sometimes. Both are gonna happen, you know."

"Is it more good than shit?"

"I think so! I'm still doing it!"

"You're doing something right!"

"I hope so!. And also, actually, that's the safest place I could be is on stage, I mean, that's the least trouble I could possibly get into! What a deal! Can I play five more minutes?"

"Talking with Robert about your songwriting, he would always bring Townes into the conversation, and talk about the two of you..."

"Well, we were best friends, and Robert – when Townes and I first met Robert, that's how we met him, together, and he went on the road and was the third member of our show, whether we were all on stage at once or doing individual sets or whatever. Townes and I were best friends for 35 years, plus I think Townes – I mean, that's the reason I started writing, even though he'd only written two songs, but, there it is, that's worth doing. Not to be like Townes, but to do that."

"Because you're not like Townes, they're different types of songs."

"Yeah, they are. And I wish I could write like that!"

Guy took a long draw from his cigarette. "Well, does Robert think I'm an asshole?"

"He thinks you're just great."

"Well, why isn't he here?! I really like Robert. He's a real gentleman, and his songs – like *The Road Goes On Forever*, it's just like, one of the best written pieces I've ever heard. When he first wrote it, man it was like, he'd come off stage and, Robert, come here and play this song, no, play it again man! He got so fuckin' tired of me, every time

I'd see him I'd drag him somewhere, get him a guitar and say to anyone I could find, listen to this, and finally Robert just went, man, leave me alone, get off of it!"

Nick said, "His songs and your songs, they both so often grab you right at the start, like Robert's *I Want to Know* – that opening line, 'Have you got a minute, a little time that we can spend?' (where is that damn guitar when you need it!) – it just takes your head somewhere else."

"Yep, well, always shoot your best shot first! Get their attention – don't hold back!"

"It's a hook, isn't it?"

"Well, I just abhor that word. It's taken on such a commercial connotation in Nashville music business, I find myself kinda cringing if it comes out of my mouth!"

"Sorry!"

"No, I can hear it from somebody else! But that's true, that's what it is..."

"The word sort of trivialises it, and it's not trivial."

"Right. I've got the original thing I wrote it down on. I've got all that – everyone of these songs. I don't know, this might be an interesting little visual -"

Guy got up from the chair and went to the closet behind him. He hunted through it for a while and then brought out two hardcover exercise books. He laid them on the table and started flipping through the early pages.

"This is before I kept anything... before I kept anything... before I kept anything..."

"Do you ever revisit them?"

"Oh, I go through them all the time when I'm looking for ideas – because I wrote everything in here, little snippets, just one line, start songs and not finish them. There, that's all the paperwork on *Old Time Feeling*, there's no other edited or, you know, worksheets or anything. But all those songs are in there. Like all of *Desperados*, the two or three pages it took to write and rewrite. You can thumb through there if you want."

He passed them over and we gingerly leafed through the priceless books containing the lyrics of all his early songs, written in his strong, slightly backward slanting, upper case hand.

"I used to write in these books, and what I found was, the books got too precious. I wouldn't write in them anymore, you know, I'd work on other pages and *then* write it in the book, and finally I thought, this defeats the purpose. Like I wrote these verses to *Heartbroke* and I wrote the chorus about 15, 20 pages apart, and I went six months or a year thinking, boy I wish I had the verses to this chorus – boy I wish I had a chorus to these verses, and one day happened to hold all the pages in between and just went huh! and that's when I started writing on separate sheets of paper!"

"Like this one: 'He was a wino tried and true' [from *Let Him Roll*] and at the bottom here you've got 'Survival's never graceful'."

"Yeah, but that's in another song."

"That's out of *Madonna With Child*."

"Yep."

"'Make no mistake' – is that what you were going to call it originally?"

"No, you can't take any of that – maybe I wrote that line down two days earlier, just had a blank page and started something else, there's no way to decipher that or make any sense of any of that kind of stuff."

As we turned the pages of the books, words and phrases from discarded songs would jump out at us. There was far too much to take in consciously, but each of hoped some of it would stick somewhere in our brains for future retrieval. Jeff thought briefly about the possibilities of hypnosis, then came back to earth. He remembered a thought he had had during the preliminary work on the project, and asked Guy, "A lot of your songs seem to work because they're almost like one-to-one conversations, they're that personal. Is that what you set out to do?"

"Yeah, because that's the kind of thing I like to read. But the thing about them is, they're about universal themes. Everybody had a grandfather or someone like that, everyone's broken something of their father's..."

Nick recognised the reference. "I can't hear *The Randall Knife* without choking up..."

"It's just a cathartic thing I wrote when my father died, probably within two weeks. And wrote it as a poem, never picked up a guitar and never thought that I would perform it as a song, a piece, it never occurred to me until later, and I couldn't figure out how to do it. I tried writing melodies – that just didn't work at all, so wound up doing it to that same guitar part as *Let Him Roll*, you know."

Then he suddenly said, "Want to see it?"

Nick and Jeff looked at each other.

"You've got it here?" said Jeff.

Guy got up from the swivel chair he'd been lounging on, went through to the office and brought the knife back, in its sheath. Nick took it out and held it gingerly. It felt so strong and right, the double curved hilt falling naturally in front of his fingers as they wrapped around the leather and bone handle.

Nick felt he was losing it a bit.

"Could I have a glass of water, Guy, I'm going a bit dry…"

"Well I guess so."

Guy's Randall Knife (Guy & Susanna Clark collection)

"Thanks very much."

He started to leave the room, then stopped in the doorway.

"I can make tea. Would you like tea?"

"Actually, yeah, that would be great. Thank you."

"Well OK, you're the first people who said yes."

"We're English, Guy."

"That's why I asked."

Some time later Guy came back into the room with a tray and all the fixings.

"You learn that in England?" Nick asked.

"No, my mother drank tea all her life. She never drank coffee, she always drank tea."

He set the tray down, sat back in his chair and picked up the knife again.

"Boy, it's a beautiful thing. And actually it was broken off, but my mother had it ground down for him, years later. And that's one of the most collectible knives in the world. Had it not been broken it's worth thousands, thousands of dollars.

"I actually have a letter from the son of the guy who made that, after his father died. *The Randall Knife* was his favourite song, and he copied the lyrics off in his own hand, off the record, and sent me a copy of it. I never did like that first recording of it [on BETTER DAYS], with drums and – I mean, I told Rodney when we did it that I didn't like it. He doesn't listen to me! That song shouldn't be done with anything but a guitar. And when it's in the right place, I'll simply unplug my guitar, walk to the front of the stage and do it with no microphone. And that's really the way it's good… but you have to do it in the right room, where people can hear."

Nick started, "The songs like *The Randall Knife* that we connect with…"

"Like I said, I think you can connect with most of my songs simply because they are universal themes – you know, like *LA Freeway*, everybody's packed up and left and it's all the little details of the stuff you leave behind."

The Middle Eighties

Guy Clark's booking agent/manager/friend is Keith Case, who runs his office from a neat wooden house nestling comfortably in amongst the modern higher-rise office buildings of all the other record companies, publishers and other businesses in Nashville's Music Row.

Keith is a friendly, outgoing (could an agent be anything else?) soul who has worked in folk and country music all his life, first in Colorado before moving to Nashville. We met him after walking all the way across the city from our motel (we are *British*, after all) on a hot, sultry day at the end of March before the water cooler season had started. He leaned back in his chair and told us about his early days in Colorado, when, from about 1967 to 1972 he ran a club presenting about 300 folk shows every year. It was during this period that he put on frequent concert presentations with Jerry Jeff Walker:

"Of course, Jerry Jeff had a reasonable sized hit with *LA Freeway* at that time and it was a major part of his show – and I don't even remember which other pieces of Guy material he did at that time but he did do a couple of other Guy songs – and so I became marginally aware of Guy primarily through that song, which I really loved. Folk music at that point in time in America was closely intertwined with the hippie movement in a lot of ways. Now that I know Guy and Susanna and know their history, the song means different things to me than it did then, but at that time it was almost like a hippie's lament – you know, getting off the LA Freeway was kind of an anthem in a way – it probably meant different forms of freedom for different listeners, but I think it had a lot of impact on people – so I guess that was the connection, which I never really thought of before.

"Anybody that was large in folk music at that time came through my room and so I became really aware of singer/songwriters and lyrics and the meanings of songs. Then a little later in the seventies when I was acting as an agent for a lot of contemporary folk and bluegrass acts I started hearing some of Guy's records at that time – Guy hadn't even made a record when Jerry was doing that song – and I was just knocked out by Guy as a songwriter and I felt he stood head and shoulders above a lot of the stuff I had been listening to all those years.

"So I actually pursued him with huge diligence for representation, which is something that I'd only done – and still to this day have only done – with one other artist. All the rest of the people I work with have come about through mutual contacts, discussions and stuff, but with Guy and John Stewart I actually went out and chased them down. And it's interesting that they're both writers who did vivid pictures of Americana in their songwriting."

Like any number of people we spoke to, Keith has a huge admiration for the way Guy crafts his songs:

"It's the way he creates these little mini-movies in his songs, the images are so strong, and when you know Guy and all his other interests – the painting, the guitar building – it all ties together. Probably in other lives he's been a cabinet builder, who knows? Partly because he's writing what he knows, and he always has, he doesn't try to delve into other areas. You know he sat in the gutter with that drunk and that he heard the drunk tell him about the Dallas whore – you know he didn't make that stuff up – but then he capsulised it and put it into this song form that creates these vivid, vivid images for people, and that's what reviewers and other artists have talked about for years about his work. Everybody talks about the craftsmanship, and it's reflected all through his work – *Boats To Build, The Carpenter, The Randall Knife*.

"I think that's a good part of his success and will probably be his legacy, and on some level it's probably like Louis L'Amour's books –

they draw a picture of a time and an era that anybody can relate to – Guy's stuff is going to be more historical later on than it is now, but a lot of his early work particularly, that ties so directly with his childhood in Texas, is a vivid picture of Texas in that time, and people relate to that.

"He brought the knife in here once – we used to do little afternoon birthday parties, when one of the agents or one of the front office people had a birthday, we'd have a cake here and all, and Guy dropped by one afternoon right when this was happening for Lee, I believe, out in the front office, and we were ready for Lee to cut the cake and Guy said, 'Just a second…' and ran out to his Scout and brought the Randall knife in – of course, I was looking for the broken tip, which has now been filed down – and Lee cut his birthday cake with the Randall knife, it just tripped me out! But the first time I heard that song, I was just devastated, and I tear up every time I hear it."

Keith also represented Townes Van Zandt before he died in 1997. We mentioned to Keith how several people – Robert Earl Keen in particular – had told us that Guy and Townes, in their songwriting as well as personally, sometimes seemed to be like two contrasting halves of the same person.

"I can see that," says Keith. "Most of Robert's contact with them was with both of them. It was a real bond, there was a very strong bond for two guys that were as different as they were from each other, and as similar as they were in some ways, and there was huge mutual respect between the two of them."

Guy Clark has had an ambivalent relationship with the music business all his working life, whether it's the record companies, publishers, promoters, agents, whatever.

Gary B. White also has a pretty jaundiced view of it: "I think Guy's one of these people, like Jerry Jeff, he's going to be more famous and more well known in their later years; I don't think either of them have been recognised by the industry in the way they should. I know when Guy first went to Sunbury Publishing out in Nashville I went over there one of the first few times I went out to visit with him, and he took me down to the basement, you know, this is my room where I write, I went, gee, that's – he says, well I signed on as a writer for hire and they're paying the rent, and I remember thinking at the time, boy, this isn't going anywhere, but it did! So at least somebody made it happen, and it must have been Guy, because I've never come across publishers that really do much more than copyright."

The business is obviously a necessary part of his career – it's what earns him a living – but he seems very disappointed at how it has let him down in various ways: taking advantage of his lack of knowledge and immaturity in the early stages, and later forcing him along career paths that he instinctively knew were wrong for him.

It is really only during the period of his last three albums, for example, that he has finally been able to adopt a way of recording that he is happy with, combined with performing in a situation he is comfortable with: either solo, with just his son Travis on acoustic bass, or using the small, tightly knit group of musicians that feature on these records. How different from the time when his first album, OLD NO.1, was released in 1975, and he went on the road to promote it:

"It just seemed kind of catch as catch can; it wasn't really organised in any sensible way, it doesn't seem like now. Seems very chaotic and stupid to me now – I mean, at one point I had eleven people on the road – roadies, keyboard players, sound guys, you know, everybody flying, renting cars – for one, two weeks it cost $35,000. That is *stupid*.

"But it was just ridiculous. Anybody who used their head would go about it in exactly the opposite way – and the perfect example is Don Williams, who went out for years and years with a bass player and a guitar player, no drums, no nothin'. And did just fine. But it was all that kind of Willie and Waylon, big band outlaw time. So that's what I tried to do. But I did not like it, I wasn't good at it. And especially at a time before the quality of electronics got good enough that you could have monitors where you could actually hear yourself with a full band around you."

Guy is realistic about the fact that playing with a band must have been good at times, especially in his younger days, but his thoughts as he grows older seem more and more to echo the words of his old Texas guitar hero, Mance Lipscomb, who said in a 1974 *Guitar Player* interview with Jim Crockett, "The electric guitar is a fraud; the sound rings because of the electricity, not because of the player. People can't remember electric songs very well either, because the music's too fast and too loud."

Whether or not Guy would agree with all of that, his attitude certainly hardened: "I hate it a lot more now than I did then, I guess I was having fun. But it got to the point where I just didn't enjoy playing the songs because I couldn't hear them, it was just way too much stuff, it cost too much money, it was too much hassle. So I quit playing for, I don't know, a year or two, and just went back to me and my guitar. I quit some time after the last Warner Brothers record, after BETTER DAYS."

In fact, there's a five-year gap in recording between BETTER DAYS and the next album, OLD FRIENDS, during which Guy continued playing the odd gig in clubs or at festivals, mostly on his own or with a few friends. One particular gig, at Kerrville in Texas in 1984, brought together on stage for the first time (but certainly not the last) Guy Clark and his young son Travis.

Travis explains: "The very first one, I played guitar with him at the Kerrville Folk Festival, the weekend of my high school graduation, 1984. That was a big weekend for me, it was really good. I wasn't playing in a band at that point, but it was a lot of fun. That was a one-off, yeah, I wasn't very good! I was alright, but looking back on it I wish I'd practised more! I knew my dad's songs, but playing them, no, not really. I was really interested in jazz, listened to a lot of Weather Report, but as far as playing goes, I was playing pop stuff, Police, U2, things like that."

After Guy and his first wife Susan were divorced, she stayed in Houston to bring up Travis, and later remarried. There was still music around, though, as Travis recalls:

"My mother plays and sings, and my stepfather is a jazz guitar player, so we always had music in the house and played a lot. I knew who my dad was, and had records and of course I'd see him, and I'd look through the records and go see him when he came; I lived in Houston in south Texas, and when he came to town of course we'd hook up and I'd see him play or whatnot, and sometimes I'd come up to Nashville and see him play here or watch him record.

"I heard a lot of jazz, and of course growing up in the late 70s, early 80s I listened to a lot of rock, I thought Van Halen was pretty much it! Once I got into high school and just out of high school I listened to the Police, a lot of reggae.

"I played trombone in junior high, through high school, then picked up the bass just because it was easier to learn to play the bass than learn how to read a completely different clef. I already read bass clef, and I played electric bass in stage bands in junior high, which was just reading old Duke Ellington charts and stuff like that, playing swing stuff. So I played trombone and bass and a little guitar. There were always guitars sitting around – my mother played guitar and piano – so I'd pick that up and plonk around on it, because it was easier to play guitar, and a whole lot easier to tune it. A piano is not something you can whup out at the campfire!"

Travis Clark would become an important part of his father's music much later, but for the moment the Kerrville gig as a duo was a one-off event. There were a number of other festivals that Guy played during this period, including Telluride and Edmonton. Holger Petersen, now head of the respected Canadian roots-orientated record

Travis & Guy on stage, c.1990 (Travis Clark collection)

company, Stony Plain, was part of the Edmonton Folk Festival organisation at the time:

"I first met Guy at the Winnipeg Folk Festival in July 1984. I was so looking forward to seeing him perform and meeting him, and it was at one of the parties at the early part of the festival. I remember exactly were he was standing and the circumstances of meeting him. My friend Richard Flohil was already talking to him and I was immediately just struck by how friendly and how warm he was – you know, he has that great smile and laugh and you feel so comfortable in his presence. For somebody like myself who revered him, it was just great to feel that, you know, within seconds you're accepted.

"So then we became fast friends and hung out together that weekend and then he gave me a copy of the BETTER DAYS cassette. At the time somehow I'd missed it when it first came out. I did an interview with him for one of my radio shows; we sat in a car while it was raining at the festival and I did the interview with him. I came back from that festival and listened to BETTER DAYS endlessly – again, it was just one of those perfect Guy Clark records, and of course with songs like *Randall Knife*, that had so much emotional impact.

"Then, in August of 84, the next month, I helped him get a booking on a TV show here in Edmonton called *Sun Country*, which was hosted by Ian Tyson – I've been working with Ian for some time – and that was a thrill. Guy and Susanna came up here, and we spent several days hanging out together.

"In 1986 I went to the Kerrville Festival and Guy and Townes were there, and ended up hanging out with them, and that was the year that Michelle Shocked recorded the TEXAS CAMPFIRE TAPES there. And in 1988 I brought her to Edmonton for a concert and I did an interview with her for my radio show. I talked to her about Guy, and she referred to him as 'God' Clark. At that point her new record was about to come out, the SHORT SHARP SHOCKED album. She described the back of the [vinyl] album as a tribute to Guy and a tribute to OLD NO.1, which has a very distinctive photo of Guy and Susanna and then hand-written song titles and credits and liner notes.

"Basically, as a tribute to Guy, she imitated it in every possible way in terms of the shading, the colours, the handwritten writing and in a very small frame in the bottom right hand corner there's a

Guy with Holger Petersen, Richard Flohil, Terry Wickham, Richard Steele, Edmonton 1994 (Edmonton Festival archive)

little thing that says 'For Guy' as her tribute.

"Anyway, she told me all about that and I mentioned it to Guy the next time we spoke. It's a very classy tribute to Guy, and I asked her, did you meet him at the Kerrville Festival, because he was there, and she said, no, she had seen Guy at Kerrville a few times, but was always just too nervous and respectful to even introduce herself. That is the kind of impact he has, you know. I think Guy's reaction to all this kind of stuff is pretty much always the same, you know, it's like, he appreciates it, he smiles and acknowledges it in a quiet way, but I don't think he takes any of it very seriously.

"So I had Guy and Townes come up for the Edmonton Folk Festival – at that point I was artistic director of the festival – the same year. And they were impressed, they really enjoyed it, and I remember the Sunday night at Edmonton Guy took me aside. When I said, I'd really like to have you come back next year, he said, well, how would you like it if I brought Rodney Crowell and Rosanne Cash? And I just about fell over thinking it might be possible to do this and he said, yeah, I think I can make it work.

"So he did, and the next year they were the closing act at the festival, and it was one of the few dates that the three of them did together on a main stage – they basically traded songs – and then I also brought in Mark O'Connor and and Jerry Douglas, and they ended up backing Rodney, Rosanne and Guy – magical, you know. It was a real special occasion. I know they did it a couple of other places around that time period, but I think he realised the festival was a songwriters' kind of event, so I was very very flattered. It was an amazing occasion.

"And I remember that weekend – I believe it was Rosanne's birthday and Guy told me they had this tradition about the three of them – or the four of them with Susanna – going out for dinner for many years on Rosanne's birthday – I may be wrong, it may have been Rodney's birthday, but I think it was Rosanne's. I suggested a really nice restaurant at the Westin Hotel in Edmonton, and unfortunately they got turned away for wearing jeans – one of those stories you just kind of shake your head about!

"But they took it pretty well, and also Guy told me they had done a few other dates as a trio, and that they loved doing it because they were so unencumbered – there were no roadies, no road managers, no backup players, just the three of them. He said at the end of the night after one of the gigs they took the money and threw it on the bed and were rolling around in the money! Because this was another thing – they didn't get paid, you know, wads of money, because it all went to road managers, so that was kind of a new experience for them."

Rodney Crowell: "Oh yes, I remember Edmonton, it was the first time I had ever seen the Northern Lights! Off and on we did some touring, and it was always really a good time. I remember Guy and Rosanne and I played a gig in Washington DC together and getting paid in cash – because it was a time when I was on the road with a band all the time, you know, accountants got the money and stuff, I never saw it – and we went back to the hotel room and threw the money up in the air! That's the first time we ever had any sense you could actually make money doing that! And Guy was saying, hey, I've been telling you all along, this is how to do it!"

In September 1989, Holger was in charge of the seminars for the Canadian Country Music Association's CCMA Week, held in Edmonton, and he put together a songwriting seminar, which was another opportunity to bring Guy up to Edmonton:

"Richard Flohil and I were in the elevator with Guy, and this singer by the name of Ronnie Prophet, who is kind of a Vegas-style country singer, got in the elevator, and looked at us, and this Ronnie Prophet is a very showbizzy, outgoing kind of guy, and then he looked at Guy Clark and I think he kind of knew that he should know him from somewhere but didn't exactly figure out who or what, but knew this guy was important. So he looked at Guy and he said, 'You seen Chet lately?' There was like a moment's silence, and Guy said, 'Not since Elmore James' funeral!' At that point the elevator door opened, and Ronnie Prophet got out, and we just rolled!

"On that occasion and a few other folk festivals, it would be such a highlight for me to hang around with Guy and a few people, other songwriters, fans, whatever, we'd go to Guy's room, and he would pull out the guitar and play stuff, his new stuff, you know, and for me that was always such a thrill, just for a handful of people to sit around listening to Guy's new songs and just totally relax with him."

During this recording hiatus, Guy was still writing songs, for himself or for other people's projects. Vince Gill had been an increasingly important figure in the last two albums, first contributing vocals to SOUTH COAST OF TEXAS, then vocals and lead guitar to BETTER DAYS, and Guy started to write with him. One of the results was the trucking song *Oklahoma Borderline*, co-written with Rodney Crowell, which Gill took into the country charts. Rodney also had hits with *She's Crazy For Leaving* and *The Partner Nobody Chose* from BETTER DAYS, both written by himself and Guy.

Rodney explains something of how the collaboration works: "We don't get to do it much, we just haven't made the time lately. But when we do it's really easy because basically we speak the same language. He's a Texas boy and I am, and our sense of humour, the things that we find funny are very similar. It's really based on characters we grew up around, and I would imagine in England it's like some of the sailors in Liverpool or wherever, the salty characters you find there. You kinda glean some of their language, the romance around who these characters are, and just the way they put words and phrases together. And mainly I guess when Guy and I get together we'll laugh a lot about stuff, we'll just start hammering around and stuff will start to take shape. One thing I always say about Guy, as a songwriter and just writer generally, he is an excellent self-editor, and one of the things I learned from him, kind of through osmosis over a period of time, is self-editing.

"I will say this as well: one of my best songwriting moves with Guy was when he came over and he had *Dublin Blues* started and he said, hey man, help me write this, and I just said no! You write that, that's yours! That was the right thing, the man who has that story and has that language should write the song."

Given the depth of appreciation for this talent shown by so many people, it's sometimes hard to understand why the name of Guy Clark isn't better known than it is. While he can still pull a large audience of devoted fans to any of his performances, his records have never sold in the quantities achieved by lesser artists and writers. From around this time in the middle eighties through to the present day, Clark has maintained a steadfastly non-populist attitude both to writing and performing. But the body of work that comprises the Guy Clark songbook has grown in stature and volume throughout his career, and Keith Case makes a valid point about this:

"He's never had any real big hits; Ricky Skaggs had a number one on *Heartbroke* – and that may be Guy's only number one, I don't know for sure – and he's had a lot of covers over the years, Vince had one on *Oklahoma Borderline*, which he and Guy wrote, but in terms of big hits he's never had that much exposure. There are songwriters in this town that have earned a zillion times what Guy Clark has earned who nobody really knows. We tried to tour one of the songwriters that had a lot of Garth Brooks' early hits; he's a wonderful performer and a great guitar player, and we tried to get him out on some shows about four, five years ago, and just had a terrible time with him.

"When we got ready to quit doing it I sat and talked with him and I said, there's such a difference between songwriters like you, who have these enormous hits but don't have a body of work that relates to you, and a Guy or a Townes, who never had any big hits but were hugely known and respected and could go out and work as performers because there was a body of work that people related with them. With these hit songwriters – who are good performers given the opportunity – their work doesn't gel into something that gives people a grasp on them as a performer.

"And some performers – like Emmylou Harris – get that identity with a body of work that isn't theirs, it's a lot of other people's work that all ties into them and the picture they're giving people on stage. A lot of artists are that way, but it isn't enough just to have a turn of phrase or such to create a batch of hit songs; Guy's material, on the other hand, creates an identity that people relate to."

Emmylou herself tells a story which gives an insight into Guy's feelings about songwriting, in particular the characters portrayed in his songs. Probably her own best known composition is *Boulder To Birmingham*, co-written with Bill Danoff as a tribute to her late singing and touring partner, Gram Parsons, and as much as anything an emotional outlet following the trauma of his death.

"I had an experience that I thought was quite interesting," she says. "This was actually just a few years ago. I was trying to do some songwriting, and I had started a song, and I wanted to see if I could try writing with the two of them [Guy and Susanna]. It was about a woman whose husband was cheating on her – very original idea! – and the idea was almost like *Your Good Girl's Gonna go Bad*, you know, it's like she was going to get on, get a life of her own.

"So we worked on it a little bit over the course of an afternoon, and then they left with the idea that we would get together at another time. A few days later I was talking to Susanna and she said, you know, Guy has a problem with this song because he says, I don't like to write songs where every character is not equal. And I thought, you're right, I never thought about that in Guy's songs, but no-one is ever better or in a stronger moral position than anyone else, and no-one is ever above anyone else. This wonderful equality, a realness of the human condition that is always there.

"It wasn't really a criticism of what I was writing, it was just where he's coming from as a writer. I wanted access to that wonderful way he has with words and how he talks about situations and puts it in a really unique way, you know, he talks about an everyday situation and makes it totally unique. But I was trying to put it into a situation that really didn't fit his deep philosophy of life which is in his writing. I mean, I've always had tremendous respect for him as a songwriter, but it gave me even more respect for him. I felt that I knew him better as a person, too. The song has still never been finished! But one day I'll finish it, and I'll try to bring some of that Guyness to it, hopefully."

Also in 1984, another young songwriter made his way to Nashville and into Guy Clark's life. Lyle Lovett is another tall, lanky Texan who grew up in Houston. Lyle explains what persuaded him to follow the footsteps of Clark, Nanci Griffith and Rodney Crowell from Texas to Tennessee:

"I had been playing the same half a dozen or so clubs around

Lyle Lovett & Guy (Guy & Susanna Clark collection)

Texas, places where I could play my own songs, for a few years. At that point in my life I was out of school and I was really trying to make a living as a musician, or as a singer-songwriter, and down in Texas there's not so much music business. Texas has always been rich in places to play, it's always had a very supportive audience, but I didn't know anything about the music business, so in 1984 I thought to myself, it's time to either learn about this and try to make a real career of this or I have to get on with something else."

Lyle had the opportunity to go to Nashville, as Nanci Griffith had invited him to put a vocal on the recording she was doing in 1984. He was aware of Nanci, being a follower of the local music, and actually met her when he was a journalism student at Texas A & M – she was coming to the University to play and Lyle interviewed her for the campus newspaper.

"So I went to Nashville," he continues, "to try to get people interested in my songs. I had done some demos and I was shocked at how friendly and receptive business people in Nashville were. I went to Nashville, I contacted ASCAP, and talked to a membership rep there, and he listened to a few of my songs on a tape and started making phone calls for me and helping me set up appointments with publishers. One of the publishers I met with was CBS Songs, where Guy was a writer. I walked in and they said I should talk to a young guy named Sam Ramage, who had grown up in Houston, then gone to school in Nashville and was working for CBS Songs. He was about my age and was a song plugger, so we were talking a little bit about our backgrounds and he mentioned that Guy Clark was one of our writers, and I told him what a great fan of Guy's I was, and that's really all I said to him.

"As a result of that he passed my tape on to Guy, in the way of, here's a kid who came in the office, said he was a fan of yours and brought this tape, check it out. And the next thing I knew, I would go back to Nashville every four to six weeks and take another round of meetings, try to meet people just to sort of see what I could see, and every time I'd go back people would say to me, oh Guy Clark played me your tape, and I thought to myself, well what the heck is going on here, and so I started hearing about Guy putting in a word for me like that before I'd ever met him! I was in shock – Guy was one of my songwriting heroes, and I was hearing stories about his passing my tape around and putting in a good word for me. I couldn't believe it, it was too good to be true."

MCA eventually signed Lyle to a recording deal. The demos he had been taking around eventually became his first album, as Tony Brown at MCA liked the tracks enough to use them. Guy wrote the brief sleeve notes to the eponymous album, including the line 'The first time I met Lyle I thought he was a French blues player.' Lyle tells of that first meeting:

"I was at lunch in a restaurant with Tony Brown from MCA and Guy was at a nearby table with Richard Leigh, and Tony took me over and I met him there at lunch, we just spoke and shook hands and that was it. He just said hello, he was very nice, and we got to know each other after that. You know, Guy had actually had a meeting with Tony – Tony told me this later – but Guy asked Tony to go to lunch with him just to give him my tape. That kind of support is just unbelievable! He wrote the liner notes on my first album, and he was referring to our first meeting. I think what he meant by that was we had been sitting across from one another, different tables in the restaurant, and from listening to my music, from knowing me through this demo tape, I didn't look the way he expected me to! He didn't think it was me, in other words; it was a surprise when Tony introduced me to him."

Guy's importance to Lyle doesn't lie simply in the helping hand he gave him in the early days, but in the example of his songwriting: "Oh, you bet. In Guy's writing, the narrative is so detailed and he conveys emotion in the best way possible by providing examples, that's what he does so well. And certainly the more I've gotten to know him over the years, the more expanded my appreciation of his work has become, as I connect up and see how – when you listen to a song like *The Randall Knife*, and you go to Guy's house and you hold that knife in your hand, it has quite an impact.

"Once again, Guy does this I think better than anybody – he's writing something very specific and detailed in his own life, yet it has universal appeal, universal meaning. Also, as a student of Guy, it shows that, gosh, you can write about something that's real – how could you imagine a story like that any better than the truth? – so in that way he lends credibility to, or shows us the importance of everyday things that happen in our lives. He teaches us to stand

Main stage, Edmonton 1989 (Edmonton Festival archive)

back and look at something that might happen during the day and be able to see the significance of it."

We asked Lyle if he had any thoughts about why Texas produces so many great songwriters. "Texas is a big place, but I do think that part of it is that writing songs is about imagination, and Texas always has been a place of imagination. It's part of the frontier mentality – go out and make it up as you go – and that independent mindset of people who are from Texas, the ability to feel as though you *can* just make something up.

"That combined with a tradition of songwriters who have gone before. I think the writers you mentioned – Butch Hancock, Terry Allen, Guy and Townes – it's because they're such great writers, because of them, and because of Bob Wills, who may have inspired songwriters like Guy and Mickey Newbury. And because of writers like Guy and Townes, younger writers were interested, so it's that tradition, and Guy and Townes are as important in that as Bob Wills, it's sort of the domino effect in a way. Jerry Jeff Walker has the perspective of someone who's not from Texas, coming here, being attracted to Texas, and I think when a person's not from a place, he sees the place with a different eye. I've lived in Texas all my life, so the fact that there *are* great songwriters in Texas doesn't seem as extraordinary as it would to someone who's from somewhere else. Texas has always been a good example of that frontier mentality, you know – Texas itself was a republic."

Texas always seems to be exerting its own gravitational force, drawing Guy Clark's thoughts and inspiration back to his roots, though Nashville has been his home for nearly thirty years. He may tell you he'd go back to live in Texas in a heartbeat, but you get the feeling there just isn't quite enough attraction to take him and Susanna back there physically. Even though the atmosphere of the city has changed and become less relaxed, and fewer evenings are spent sitting in with other players, still there are too many of their friends around to make the move likely anytime soon.

But in the 1980s, when Guy Clark's career seemed to be in the balance, it's easy to imagine that there was a critical moment when he could have simply decided to up and leave. Typically, he sums up the whole period of uncertainty in a succinct sentence or two: "Yeah, there's like five years between BETTER DAYS and OLD FRIENDS, when I just quit playing with the band, pretty much quit playing and decided to just make an acoustic record, or learn how. Mostly I was just trying to figure out what to do."

What he eventually figured out, as far as recording went, was just to do it by himself. But then he met Miles Wilkinson again.

MILES

MILES Wilkinson is a soft-spoken Canadian from Toronto, who has been an important and integral part of the Guy Clark story for more than ten years.

Fellow Canadian Holger Petersen first met him in Los Angeles when visiting his friend Bob Hunka, also from Edmonton, who was Brian Ahern's partner in Happy Sack Productions – they produced Emmylou Harris' first record.

"I was fortunate enough," says Holger, "on my occasional trips to LA, to see that come together and to go to the odd session and record release party, and to meet the people that were around that scene and in Emmy's band. That's how I met Miles Wilkinson – Miles comes up here quite a bit, and we've worked on records together with Cindy Church and Long John Baldry."

Miles remembers how he first came across Guy: "I was working many years ago in Toronto with Brian Ahern, who had been producing Anne Murray for years; I was working as an engineer and also playing guitar for her. Then in the early seventies Brian, who had done about ten Anne Murray albums at the time, built this recording studio, the Enactron Truck, in a semi trailer, and started working with Emmylou Harris – he ended up, among other things, marrying Emmylou.

"Now around that time this young unknown songwriter came to Brian's attention; his name was Rodney Crowell, and Brian signed Rodney to a publishing deal. Rodney came to Toronto on a number of occasions; Rodney and I became friends, and Rodney introduced me to Guy Clark's music. Rodney always talked about, you know, Guy was the person who taught him how to be a songwriter. And it wasn't long after that that Brian's truck and his whole production operation moved to Los Angeles.

"I stayed in the Anne Murray band for about another year, then I kinda got bored with it and decided I was more interested in what goes on in the studio. So a year after Brian went to LA I followed him down there, and through Rodney met Guy who was staying there at the time. And I remember just spending hours in the evening in my bedroom listening to Guy Clark a lot, just really being taken by the songwriting.

"I guess it was the stories – somehow they just rung something in me. See, I grew up with rock'n'roll, I was in a band that played a lot of Beatles and Beach Boys, Stones and stuff like that, and this whole sort of country, singer/songwriter thing was all very new to me. And of course working on the Emmylou records was a great education for that. I was exposed to a lot of music, but the Guy Clark records, I just played them over and over again.

"Then at the same time Rodney took me to the Troubadour one night to see Willie Nelson play, who I had never heard of in my life, and everybody there in the Troubadour was, you know, this person's God and I had never heard of the guy! I mean, I was completely ignorant of this stuff. But the great thing about being with Brian over these years was I was getting introduced to country music at an extraordinarily high level – you know, Emmylou and all the other stuff that Brian was doing at that time was – not only was it the best that there was, but it was also extremely innovative. Those early Brian records had a huge effect on the country music business.

"So I was getting educated by the players, by these great artists, so that was really something, and as I said I had met Guy and had spent a little bit of time with him in social situations. Brian Ahern had leased a house in Beverly Hills where the truck was housed and we recorded a lot of those albums right there in the house with the truck sitting outside.

"There was a group of us affectionately called the Brian Ahern School of Recording! An enormous number of influential people came out of that, including Tony Brown and Rodney and Emory Gordy, really just an amazing list of people that were connected, initially on the Emmylou projects, then on other things like Willie Nelson's *Stardust* album. Brian didn't produce that, but the truck was hired and among other people I was one of the engineers. It would be easy to say it was the best period of my life – I've had a lot of other great times, but it was pretty exciting, and I was really young. And yet, as I said, I would spend hours listening to Guy's stuff and just enjoyed it.

"Anyway, I longed to pursue my producing career, and after several years down there, I had a friend who was a manager and agent for some authors of the time, in particular Tom Robbins, her name was Phoebe, and one day she said to me, 'acorns don't grow under great trees'! And I got to see that I'd gone probably about as far as I was ever going to go being in the Brian Ahern crowd.

"So I took a big leap of faith and went back to Toronto and spent a couple of years trying to figure out how I could get my US immigration organised. With that done and being able to be in the States, I ended up in Minneapolis and spent some time there really getting my engineering chops together, out from the shadow of Brian Ahern and that whole gang of people, because in LA there was a team of us that worked together, four engineers that would work around the clock to keep up with Brian! And Brian was an engineer also. And I just really wanted to pursue my own producing career and I just realised I was going to have to jump out of that on my own, you know, like the student finally leaves the mentor.

"So then I got to be a partner in a studio in Minneapolis and really worked on my engineering and got into a jazz circle, recorded a lot of jazz as well as what was called at the time new wave rock'n'roll, and decided after being there for about five years that it was time for me to go back to Los Angeles. And I discovered that practically everybody that I knew in LA had moved to Nashville!

"In this business so much of it is who you know, and I realised that I knew practically nobody any more in LA and most of the people I knew were in Nashville. So I made an exploratory trip, and decided that it would be a good thing, and made the jump and moved here. And that would be, I think around '85. Now I wasn't here very long when I got a phone call from Guy Clark! Because of course I looked up the people I knew and one of the first I looked up was Rodney Crowell.

"So Guy calls me and he tells me that he has signed a publishing deal with, at the time it was CBS Publishing, and that they had a run-down little 8-track studio that was a mess, and he said, nobody uses it, and the few times anybody tries to use it it's always terrible! Guy remembered me from the LA days; he said, I always really liked you, and I think maybe you should fix this studio, we can maybe figure out if we can make this thing work. Somehow I had made an impression upon him and Susanna, and I was really surprised because even though I'd met Guy a few times I had no idea that he'deven remember who the heck I was!"

Guy went over with Miles to look at the small rundown CBS studio and discovered that the basic components were pretty good, but it was just put together very badly – especially the wiring. They did a few recording sessions in it and then talked CBS into getting them some money to tear it all away and rewire it.

Miles had been working with Guy for about a year, making publishing demos in the studio, when Guy mentioned that he had a dream of making a kind of record that he'd never made before but had always wanted to make. Miles recalls:

"Guy said, first of all, all the records he had made at that time were kind of typical Nashville produced records. Even though it was another era than it is now, it was still sort of the formula that gets sometimes called the cookie-cutter formula, using Nashville players and doing it in a particular way, using particular instruments – his records had been like that before, and he had a lot of fun making them, but he just never felt they were really true to his visions of the songs.

"And he had gotten to a point in his career where he had almost felt he'd had his recording career, it was over, and he was a songwriter now, a respected songwriter, and he felt that he deserved to make the kind of record he wanted to make, even though it was obviously going to be a very low-key, low budget project. So we came up with some rules for what this vision should be.

"The rules were that, first of all we would base the entire music around his guitar parts. That was a very radical, different thing – we completely reversed the way he had been treated before. Another rule was that there would be no fades – every song would have an organic, real ending – and no reverb, because for him that was a fake thing. I mean, a good word for Guy is organic, everything is based on reality, on the earth. And the last rule was there would be no electric instruments of any kind, it would be strictly acoustic. So, armed with those ideas, we started talking about it and thinking about it.

"Another thing I discovered very quickly doing the demos was that Guy could never play the song twice in a row – it was just a waste of time to do it the second time because there was no performance. The moment he had to repeat it, all that was magical about the song was gone, and you could just tell he was thinking it rather than feeling it. There was no communication of the poetry, and the thing I was wanting from Guy in the work I was doing, working for a publishing company, was the importance of the songs and the importance of really communicating the songs.

"At first I couldn't figure out how in the world we could do it, but I was so determined to work with him and to come up with something that I never really thought, this is impossible, it was like, how do we figure this out?

"I will tell you that the vast majority of this was Guy's ideas, you know, I was just helping him figure out how to do it. Remember we had this publishing deal, and before we made the record I had recorded maybe 50 songs of his as the publishing engineer – we used that time to build our relationship, so by the time we got to doing that, the record wasn't that difficult. The biggest problem we had was in the mixing end of it.

"Anyway we came up with this idea that we would decide what the ten songs were and write a set list and he would come into the studio on the weekend – the publishing company studio that we had rewired – and he would play a set. And then he would leave! We'd do that on the weekend, so he'd come in on Saturday around noon, and since it was just him and guitar we were recording, the setup was very easy, you know, a few microphones, and recorded the set. And the next day he'd come back, and we'd do the same thing. And we did that on weekends for a couple of months.

"Essentially he was treating it like another gig. We might stop the tape between tunes sometimes, sometimes we wouldn't – the idea is that he'd only have to play the song once each time."

"And we did that for several months, and at the end of this period of time we had one take of ten songs that we felt that the timing was pretty good, the performance was exactly the type of performance he wanted, and he sang well, you know, so we edited it together, the very best takes, and at that point, once we edited those together, we then brought in some guests and friends and added a few things. We were only working on eight tracks at the time, and in fact the working title for that album was 'Less is More, More or Less'. The idea was that if we ever filled up eight tracks on the tune the tune was finished!

"So we kept it very very simple, and really only added a few things on some songs. Verlon Thompson was playing on the sessions, of course. Rodney came in and sang on a couple of things, then Emmylou came in and, let's see, Rosanne of course, and Vince Gill. Very little percussion, we brought in Kenny Malone to play a couple of little percussion parts, mostly congas, and then Guy did a few funny little things, I can't remember what they were,we banged knives or whatever, you know. Just a very organic kind of thing.

"And before we got a chance to mix that record CBS Songs was bought up by the new company SBK that was formed – they came in and bought up publishing companies all over the world and CBS Songs was one of them. So we moved to another building and we moved our little rewired 8-track setup over to this other building and then we mixed it over there. We mixed it digitally – this was in the early days of digital mixing.

"Guy and I had two disagreements on that record! The first concerned the title song, *Old Friends*; I remember when we recorded the original demo for that song, I was in this tiny control room and out in the studio floor – this was the demo, so there were a few players, we'd been working with these organic sounds, acoustic sound. And we had a guy named Biff Watson on guitar and a bass player, Dave Pomeroy. But nobody had ever heard the song, and Guy just goes up there and plays it with essentially no rehearsal.

"And these guys are great players, and they just sort of play along. And at the end of the song I stopped the tape and there was absolute silence in the room. And there was, you know, a tear rolling down my eye, and we were all just stunned at this song, and I remember the first thought that went through my head was, that was the single most intimate song and performance I had ever heard in my life. It was this incredible sense of intimacy. And the way the song was written is that anyone could really apply it directly to themselves, you know, the importance of old friends in their lives, and that is the most important thing in the world.

"So of course I was very happy when Guy wanted to put that song on the record. The disagreement that we had came up when we were working on the overdubs – as I said, we only added a few little things to each song, or some of the songs. Well, Guy really wanted Emmylou on the song, and from day one I remember feeling, I don't think that's right, because the moment you add another voice to that song it no longer becomes a communication between Guy and you, the listener – it's between Guy and this other person he's singing with. It moves it one step of intimacy away – it's no longer about you, the listener. And I expressed that to him, and he said, well, okay, I understand that but I know Emmy will put this incredibly beautiful part on it. I said, well, I'm not debating that at all, I just don't know if I agree with the idea.

"And we had that disagreement all the way through the making of the rest of that record. And Emmylou did come in and of course sang amazingly well, phenomenally – it was a brilliant harmony part – but from that moment on to me the song may have sounded a little better, but it lost some of the magic, because it was no longer communicating.

"All the way through, even to the mastering of the record, I kept bringing it up and – you see, I have this philosophy about producing – my name is not the biggest name on the record, so it's not my record! And a lot of the ideas I get as a producer, I'm not really attached to at all, it's just an idea like anybody else's. I throw it out and if it's a good idea, great, and if it isn't I don't really care. Once in a while I'll come up with something I really do feel is important, and the artist will know that by my persistence. Not that I'll get angry or mad about it, but if I feel strongly about it I'll just keep bringing it up. But I will always, absolutely always, bow to the artist in the end.

"So anyway, at the end when we listened to the whole thing played back he said, well, you know, how do we like it? I said, Guy, I think it's great except for one thing! And he said, that's okay! We even mixed both versions, because I was so persistent, but the version with Emmy is what ended up on the record.

"Now the other disagreement we had was that Guy had always felt his vocal had been too buried on his previous records, and the songs suffered as a result – for Guy there is nothing more important than the song – and this is one of the reasons why he didn't want any reverb, but the other thing is he really wanted that vocal to be upfront. Well, when we were mixing the record, I'd get the song sounding where I wanted and then he would actually sit down at the console and push around some of the faders!

"And basically, to make a long story short, I agreed with him that his vocals should be louder than his previous records, but I did not agree with him about how loud he was making his vocal. And I couldn't get through to him on that and I would say, I'd tell him, look, I've made a cassette of this and put it in my car, and the vocal is so loud the wind noise driving down the street would block out all the music! I sympathise with you, but you've got to hear the music. Well, again, in the end it's his record, you know, so we ended up using the mixes he wanted.

"Now about six months after the record was released Guy comes back from one of his many trips on the road and he tells me that he was in Gilley's, huge Country club in Fort Worth. And he said, well Miles, I went into this club and they were playing my record, and you were right, I couldn't hear anything but my vocal, just could not, the bar sounds and the people, just completely wiped out all the music. So he said, from now on you don't let me anywhere near the console! I trust you, you know, you do that job. It was a big moment.

"I'd still have worked with him, absolutely, because I love Guy Clark and I would be there for him. I mean, I'll be honest with you, Guy Clark doesn't sell a lot of records, we don't make a lot of money, but the rewards of being there when this music gets recorded are just so great, that takes precedence over all that other stuff."

Old Friends

So in 1988, Guy went in with a batch of ten songs – for the first time, the majority of which were either co-written or written by other people – to record his 'comeback' album, Old Friends. The LP was released in 1989 on U2's Mother Records; the members of U2 had become Clark fans while they were recording in America. Guy sums up his view of the rationale behind the making of the record:

"Like I said, I had to go back and relearn how to do what I wanted to do, just not listen to anybody else, just do what I thought was right. And, with the help of Miles Wilkinson, who's the engineer and co-producer – he's just a wizard in the studio, has excellent ears – he gets it on tape and I decide what we're going to do and how we're going to do it."

The track that hits you hardest on first hearing is not one of Guy's at all, but *Come From the Heart*, a brief, simple song with an irresistible chorus:

You got to sing like you don't need the money
Love like you'll never get hurt
You got to dance like nobody's watchin'
It's got to come from the heart if you want it to work

Keith Case tells how impressed both he and Guy were with the song: "You know, Susanna co-wrote *Come From The Heart* with Richard Leigh, and Guy carried a tape of that song, right before he did OLD FRIENDS, which was ten years ago. We talked about that song all the time, Guy and I did, because we both felt this song was just a stone cold smash, and it was really funny because Guy kept saying, Susanna won't let me cut it! You know the song hadn't been cut at that point and they obviously were looking for a major country act to have a big hit on it and make a lot of money.

"I presume that if Guy had really wanted to cut it he certainly could have, but at least he carried around this story that Susanna wouldn't let him cut it, because various country artists kept holding it and stuff, and of course Guy and I were encouraging the world to cut it, we both just were so secure in the thought that it was a hit, and then Kathy Mattea cut it and it was an enormous hit for her, but I could never hear that song without thinking about Guy, it definitely expresses how he thinks about songwriting."

Guy adds: "The first time I heard it I thought, wow, what a great piece of writing! She and Richard Leigh wrote it in like, 45 minutes or something. Kathy Mattea was going to do it. They had it on hold, and having never been recorded the controller of the copyright can withhold that licence to record if they have a star who's going to cut it. But it all worked out timing-wise. Believe me, I wouldn't have hurt Kathy's sales at all!"

Guy also collaborated with Richard Leigh on one song, *All Through Throwin' Good Love After Bad*, a mid-tempo four-step which on the album didn't turn out quite how it was written: "There's two versions of that song. Mine is in 4/4, like a bluegrass tune, but we originally wrote it in 6/8, like a Ray Charles song, and Tammy Wynette recorded it like that. That's the way the song was originally written, and I just couldn't do that, couldn't sing it like that. Richard can, like Ray Charles would have done."

Of the album's other songs, *To Live is To Fly* is a lovely Townes Van Zandt song that Guy often plays live, along with *Watermelon Dream*, a Jesse Winchester-like snapshot of a hot, lazy Southern evening; *The Indian Cowboy*, by Guy's old Texas friend Joe Ely, is a waltz time tale of a circus disaster that was originally recorded for the SOUTH COAST OF TEXAS album, but never made it on to vinyl; and

Guy with Willie Nelson and Johnny Cash, BMI awards Nashville c.1990 (Beth Gwinn)

Heavy Metal Don't Mean Rock'n'roll To Me is about a construction worker and his love affair with his D-10 bulldozer: fairly atypical macho stuff, and perfect, you might think, for Johnny Cash, who indeed covered it on his Is Coming To Town album.

But the finest song on the album is *Immigrant Eyes*, co-written with Roger Murrah, telling the story of a young man, 'confused and alone', arriving in New York at the turn of the century:

Oh Ellis Island was swarming
Like a scene from a costume ball
Decked out in the colours of Europe
And on fire with the hope of it all...

Sometimes when I look in my grandfather's immigrant eyes
I see that day reflected and I can't hold my feelings inside...

The song closes with the old man at the end of his life and, while it may not reach the heights of literacy and understanding of the great Guy Clark songs of old age – *Let Him Roll, Old Time Feeling, Desperados* – it is nevertheless a moving statement of gratitude from one generation to another.

The amount of collaboration in Guy Clark's songwriting has been substantial during the past few years. The list of co-writers is extensive: apart from those previously mentioned, like Vince Gill, Rodney Crowell and Keith Sykes, it also includes Jay Booker, Shawn Camp, David Allan Coe, Roger Cook, Charlie Craig, Stewart Harris, John Lloyd, Steve Wariner, Pam Tillis and Lori Yates. Most of these are Guy getting involved with other people's projects, and some of the songs seem to have very little Guyness about them, but they are still important in helping to maintain the flow, and those which end up on Guy Clark albums are generally a cut above the others.

Looking at it overall, OLD FRIENDS is a transitional album – whilst the sound of the record is wonderful in its acoustic simplicity, and Guy's voice seems better than ever, the songs are just not as strong as could be expected after such a long layoff, and another three years was to pass before the true return to form with the magnificent BOATS TO BUILD.

Boats To Build

After the Old Friends album, the nineties arrived, CDs took over completely from LPs, the time stretched out further and further and we thought maybe that really *was* it with Guy Clark albums, and that was to be his slightly disappointing swansong. Then out of the blue in 1992 came news of a new recording, and we waited and waited until finally the little plastic cases arrived in the London stores.

Boats To Build, it said on the front cover in an antique typeface below a stern sepia photograph of Guy, his head tilted questioningly to the right. We slipped the dark green disc into the CD player and rocked back on our heels as the joyful sound of *Baton Rouge* danced out of the speakers like a long-delayed second helping of *Texas Cookin'*. The smiles on our faces grew wider song by song as this wonderful music filled the room. Every track was a jewel: we were building boats with Guy, plucking mandolins courtesy of Picasso, and crawling out from behind the couch alongside Larry Mahan. Never mind that the Tories had just won yet another general election – Guy Clark was back and all was right with the world.

During the making of Old Friends, the differences of opinion between Miles Wilkinson and Guy had led to the final working out of what their working relationship was, and they talked about a record that both of them someday wanted to make – a re-recording of some of Guy's great older songs, but with the new acoustic sound and instrumentation they had been working towards. This ultimate goal was not to be reached for another five or six years, but in the summer of 1991 Guy had enough songs gathered together to start recording again. Miles takes up the story:

"We kept talking about this over and over again. Nevertheless we then made the BOATS TO BUILD record, and we put this small band together with Kenny Malone on drums and Verlon Thompson on second guitar and I thought it was going to be really great. And then he announced he wanted his son to play bass. And I didn't even know he had a son! So all of a sudden I'm going oh my God, what is this going to be! And I was pretty worried about it.

"Well, we'd kept talking about we would never bring anyone on a record unless the song really called for it, and there was always that balance between, okay, do we have all Guy's friends who are big famous people in the business coming in to guest on the record, or do we make the record for the sake of the record? There was always this sort of debate would go on, and we would try to find the middle ground there. But when he wanted Travis to play on it, it was, oh God, what are we in for now?

"Well, of course, Travis came in and was wonderful! And that took care of that! So we made that record, and true to his word, Guy never came anywhere near the console, he let me do my stuff. And we made that record, we were very happy, and it's like every record we did we added a new element."

Travis Clark hadn't played very much with his father since that first time at the Kerrville Festival in 1984, but in 1990 had a call from Guy asking if he would like to go to Italy; this eventually led to the BOATS TO BUILD recording and playing regularly together: "I was playing in a kind of a reggae rock band in Texas, doing that full time, just playing a whole lot, and my dad heard me play a couple of times, and I sent him tapes, and I guess from hearing what I was doing with that band and realising that I could probably pick up, you know, any sort of style, he realised I might be able to help him out.

"So he called me one time, he had a gig in Italy, and needed the band, and the band was me and Verlon, just a 3-piece. He came down and we played as a duo in Fort Worth and left the next day to go to Torino to play a one-nighter – on my first wedding anniversary!

"That show was really really good – it was some sort of festival, and the headliner was Jerry Lee Lewis! What a pairing! It was in a big basketball arena, Barry and Holly Tashian were there as well – it was interesting. I don't know, it just went really well, it was just like, wow, this is pretty neat. And it seemed that we might need to do that more often, so from that point for I guess about a year, year and a half, whenever he would come to Texas – because I was still playing in my band, it was my full-time job – or whenever logistically it worked out we would play together. I had to cancel some things, but it worked out best, you know. Then later we hooked up on a more regular basis. It wasn't me that decided, you know, that ball would be in his court. He asked, and I said, definitely, by all means, I'd love to play, whenever it works out logistically, and whenever you can afford it! And then I moved up to Nashville in February 1992, and we kind of decided to make a deal of it.

Travis and Guy on stage c.1992 (Travis Clark collection)

"But we recorded BOATS TO BUILD the year prior to that, in the summertime. Now that was a lot of fun, actually getting up here and playing with those players, that calibre of players, and in a real studio. The things I'd done before, I'd recorded with my little band, and that was mediocre and I was not real tickled with the product, but playing with that calibre of players and the calibre of songs we were playing, it was something else."

We asked Travis about his own favourite song: "Oh, the opening cut, *Baton Rouge*, that's hard to beat! I mean, to me, you couldn't ask for a better opening lick. It's right there, it really is. When I was on the road a lot, people would often tell me, man, I like BOATS TO BUILD better than I like DUBLIN BLUES. They're two completely different feels, but of course the thing that sticks in most people's mind about BOATS TO BUILD is gonna be that opening riff, it's just a killer."

The title track of the album is a beautiful, slow, rolling tune with muffled cymbals providing echoes of waves gently crashing on the shore:

Sails are just like wings
The wind can make them sing
Songs of life, songs of hope
Songs to keep your dreams afloat

I'm gonna build me a boat with these two hands
It'll be a fair curve from a noble plan
Let the chips fall where they will
I've got boats to build

Guy says, "Verlon and I actually wrote the song for Richard Leigh, who's a wooden boat builder and sailor. Richard's the guy who wrote *Don't It Make My Brown Eyes Blue* and wrote *Come From The Heart* with Susanna. Anyway, for a birthday present his wife had given him two weeks at the boat building school at Maine – classic wooden boats. Richard was off building wooden boats, and Verlon and I said, boy, I really miss old Richard, I bet he's having a great time, let's write him a song.

"I worked in the boatyard as a summer job when I was in high school, and one year after I got out, I worked on a big sailboat for a year or something. But the neat thing about boats is – building houses, everything's gotta be square, but boats are all curves, and it's what they call 'square with the world' – not square with anything *but* the world!"

Again, all but two of the songs on the album were written jointly with various other people, but the feeling you get, especially from reading the lyrics, is that Guy's contribution is more substantial than with the co-written songs on OLD FRIENDS. Guy explains about the increasing amount of collaboration on the last few records:

"It just evolved, from getting stuck, getting tired writing by yourself, wanting to do something different. Sometimes it's fruitful, sometimes it's not. Most of the time when I write with other people it's for their project, or something other than my own albums. But once in a while something will come of that.

"Sometimes we'll sit down together, sure, or maybe someone will come with an idea. A lot of the time Rodney and I write together with things that we've started and we don't know where they go. So we have a pretty good chunk of it, but don't know where to take it."

Picasso's Mandolin was written with Radney Foster and Bill Lloyd, who had many country hits as a duo in the eighties. It's a song Guy prefers even to *Boats to Build*:

"The story behind that is that I got real taken with wanting to play the mandolin, so I went and bought the cheapest mandolin I could find that looked like a mandolin, you know. Made in Korea, had the curlicues and the f-holes and everything, very cheap, and I was writing with Foster and Lloyd one day and the mandolin was sitting in the corner.

"I had a couple of puffs and a couple of drinks and was just looking at that mandolin, and just went goddamn man, you know that mandolin looks like the Koreans got a painting by Picasso of a mandolin and used it for the plans! They did, when you look at it closely it's just a little exaggerated here and out of shape, and it's just like, man that's what it is. And we laughed about it and all of a sudden it was like, there's a song! It's not just the physical shape of the mandolin, it's the metaphor for playing on Picasso's mandolin, you know – no rules! So that's how that song came about."

Guy has known Ramblin' Jack Elliott for some twenty years, since Jack, not a native Texan, based himself in Austin; Guy wrote the liner notes for Jack's SOUTH COAST album, as well as being part of his recent FRIENDS OF MINE record that Susanna mentions in her conversation (and for which she wrote the liner notes). *Ramblin' Jack and Mahan* sounds like a Texas version of an epic poem – a tale of one party night that has gone down in legend.

Stayin' up all night at the Driskill Hotel
Ramblin' Jack and Mahan, cowboyed all to hell,
And the room smelled like snakes and the words sound like songs
Now there's a pair to draw to boys, I would not steer you wrong

Jerry Jeff Walker tells of the background behind what have been a big part of the Austin music scene for many years now, the March Birthday Parties:

"1980 was my 40th birthday, and we decided to do something big

Guy & Jerry Jeff Walker, backstage, Edmonton 1989 (Edmonton Festival archive)

in Austin for the environment – Austin sits on top of one of the biggest aquifers in central Texas, and to keep construction from building right over the top of it there's been this environmental movement for a long time called The Spirit of the City. So we decided to have a musical day to raise money for that organisation, and all the bands in Austin would come and play, we set it up right down by the spring. I had a Fun Run in the morning and as soon as it ended I went on stage and we played from noon until midnight, one band right after another, and it was a lot of fun, and that became the start of the birthday deal.

"We went indoors after that to a concert hall – my wife said people might like to sit down for a while after standing in the sun all day. And so we started doing them in there, and instead of people bringing their bands I would invite some of my friends who play all year long – just bring your wife and your guitar and come down, we'll swap songs on stage, so we set the stage up like a big bar and people would be honorary bartenders – my dad's been a bartender, the governor's been a bartender.

"And everybody sits on stage and watches each other, you know, Mickey Newbury, Guy Clark, Harlan Howard, those kind of people, and they take turns getting up and playing and it's been a fun event. And then usually on Sunday I take everybody to Luckenbach for a dance with my band. It's a lot of fun and bands come from all over the country – anybody can play so there's a hotelful of people partying and playing guitars, quite a festive deal."

Holger Petersen was at the 1991 Birthday Party: "I happened to be in Austin during the South By South West music convention when Jerry Jeff's Birthday Party coincided with that event. That was at the Driskill Hotel, which is like the cowboy hotel in Austin. It's a magical kind of place, you know, LBJ used to have his office there, it's a huge Texas hotel and there was a big party that night, and that was the occasion Guy wrote about in *Ramblin' Jack and Mahan* – well, I was there in the early stages of that party. I left before people started crawling out from behind couches, but it was great to then see something like that surface as a song!"

The construction of the song was not as straightforward as it might seem, says Guy: "That came about in an interesting way. Richard Leigh and I were writing and had written those verses, and weren't sure what it was about or what the chorus was, and just kinda got stuck and put them away for several months and didn't work on it. And I had gone down to Jerry Jeff's birthday, and gone through this little scene with Jack and Mahan, you know, staying up all night, and I started writing that chorus, and all of a sudden I snapped those verses went with it, with a little bit of rewriting. And Richard said okay!"

Rodney Crowell is the co-writer of *Jack Of All Trades*: "I think Guy always had a fondness for my father, he was a construction worker and a hillbilly singer, my dad would drink Old Crow whiskey and I think Guy just had a fondness for the character that he was, and I think that's what's kinda borne out of – basically my dad was this jack of all trades and I think it was a combination of my dad and just other people we grew up around."

How'd You Get This Number, co-written with Susanna, is for anyone who's ever had a boring, unwanted caller on the other end of the telephone. The verses are what's actually said out loud and the chorus is what you really want to say: "I can't remember how that came about – it's just a funny song – I'm sure it was somebody, some asshole I'd obviously gotten drunk and given my phone number to! Call me anytime! I mean, there's nobody to blame in any of these songs but me! I'm not throwing the blame on anybody – I'm owning it!"

The remaining tracks on the album are barely less strong. *Madonna with Child ca. 1969* was an old song which again had been recorded as a demo for the SOUTH COAST OF TEXAS album, and harks back to Guy's spell in San Francisco around that time. He admits the song is about someone real, but won't say who, or anything about the circumstances.

I Don't Love You Much Do I is a nicely ironic ('just more than anything else in this whole world') love song, again written with Richard Leigh, with Emmylou taking a verse and putting some typically beautiful harmonies on the chorus; and *Too Much*, co-written with Lee Roy Parnell, is an ode to moderation with some juicy couplets, like:

Too much hot rod'll get you a ticket
Too much dog'll make you kick it and

Too much chip'll bruise your shoulder
Too much birthday'll make you older

One of the more unexpectedly impressive things about the album is the sound; most Guy Clark albums have had a production quality that fitted in well with Guy's voice and were good of their type and for their time, but BOATS TO BUILD (and DUBLIN BLUES which followed) sounds ezquisite. The instruments and vocals are clear, deep and warm; it should be required listening for anyone attempting to record an acoustic album. Travis Clark puts it best:

"Really, it's *not* produced! The sound is very representative of what Guy wants to do, and has wanted to do forever. It's the organic thing – wood, strings, fingers. You know, one of the funniest things Miles says, he likes to spend half a day in the studio trying to get that perfect reverb, you know, that living room kind of sound. And then turn it off! And, you know, when we played live, much to everybody's surprise, especially all the engineers, we'd say, whatever that is, turn it off – whatever that thing is, compression, reverb, any of it, we don't want any of it! If it's not coming out of us at that point in time, we don't want it coming out. Because it's all about right then, the music that you get is the music that we're feeling right then – that's the art part of it as far as I'm concerned."

Between the recordings, Guy was continuing to tour, but still by no means as extensively as in his earlier career, and sometimes made time to be involved in other peoples' projects. One such, in 1993, was Nanci Griffith's 'back to the folk roots' album OTHER VOICES, OTHER ROOMS, on which Guy joins Nanci singing a Woody Guthrie song about the migration to a new life in California. Nanci tells of the perils of promotional shows:

"He's just a great pal, you know, Guy and I have worked together so much, and he was a major part of the first volume of OTHER VOICES, OTHER ROOMS, with he and I doing Woody Guthrie's song *Do Re Mi* together. For the second volume, OTHER VOICES TOO, we brought all the Texas 'brat pack' of writers in to do *Desperados Waiting For a Train*, of course mainly Rodney Crowell and Jimmie Dale Gilmore, Eric Taylor, and Steve Earle and Guy, but with that first record we did a tour and a documentary film.

"We were filming the documentary, we were in Austin playing at the Paramount, and we had about 15 guests that had to be woven in and out of the show, Guy being one of them. And we didn't have a music director, just me and Jim Rooney and my band, the Blue Moon Orchestra.

"And everything was running smoothly, you know, with Emmylou and everybody. Then Guy came out and we were rehearsing *Do Re Mi*, and Guy was playing it in what I thought was a different key to what we'd recorded it. And he said, no, this is what we recorded it in. And you know, I just said, oh Guy, do you know I've gone all this time without a music director, and now it has to be you I'm in conflict with!

"It was hilarious – Guy got mad at me and I got mad at Guy, and both of us exited opposite sides of the stage, and when I came off the stage Jim Rooney said, Nanci, Guy was right – it had been in C, I think – and I went, oh dear God what a terrible day, now I have to go

Guy with Nanci Griffith, c.1992 (Guy & Susanna Clark collection)

out there and apologise to Guy Clark! I did, of course, but of all the people for me not to realise what key something was in, it had to be Guy, because he and I had so naturally sung it in the studio without any rehearsal at all. And it was just funny working with all these other people, some of whom are notoriously difficult, and me and Guy were the two people that had to bump heads over that!"

Guy and Travis were now starting to play more regularly together. As well as playing his acoustic bass guitar, Travis was also contributing strong vocals: "I'd been singing in the reggae band. Me and the guitar player would swap off; the guitar player sang most of it but I started picking up and trying to sing more, just to change it around so you don't have a totally predictable sound.

"Playing with my dad, it came naturally. I didn't think about it at first, and then the more I would analyse it, people would say wow, why are you doing that, and I would go, I don't know! But to be real honest, a lot of the high notes, the only way I could hit those notes is by singing really loud or hoarse. One of the things I like to do, it sounds kinda weird: if you were to hear me sing back up on some of his kinda love songs, I may sound kinda growly, still high end but a little coarse maybe. For some reason I like totally different textures, like one person singing in falsetto and then another person underneath that volumewise, giving it a different feel."

"From a musical point of view it was freedom. Playing my dad's stuff I was given free rein, you know, he never ever told me what to play, he just gave me a framework and I could play anything I wanted, so it was total freedom.

One of the things that makes a Guy Clark performance special, particularly in more recent times, is the extent to which each performance of a song feels unique, almost as if it's the first time it's been played. We asked Travis if that was difficult to fit into.

"It could be, but as a duo, you have so much room, and you both know generally how the song goes. We'll call that a given, you have to start there. But from there Guy could express himself in any way that he chooses on that night, and I could express myself in any way that I choose on another night. I'll be real honest, sometimes it clashed. Not real often, but sometimes it did. Musically sometimes it would go *wow!* – we'll try not to do that again! I'd say 90-95% of the time it would be pretty spectacular. I had tapes, but we didn't ever rehearse; the only rehearsals we've ever done were maybe 4 or 5 hours prior to a recording.

"It probably does have something to do with the fact that we're related, I think there's some validity to that point. It's something I couldn't explain, and as a Darwinist I'm looking for something to explain! But it would be hard to put your finger on. I'm sure it must be – look at the Everly Brothers!

"The musical relationship has certainly brought us closer – I actually got to spend some time with him, where I definitely hadn't in the early years. I mean, we lived in different states. But you spend that much time with someone, you wind up being friends, learning more about him, and getting an insight into some of the ways that he would write, and some of the isms he had about music in general. And that also helps the performance – if I know that he feels a certain way about a song, or thinks to himself, this is the mood I wanted in this when I wrote it, you kind of get a feeling of how it might be played. Or it might change the way you feel about playing it, and give it a different twist."

Also in 1993, and about eighteen months after BOATS TO BUILD, Guy and Travis came over to London and played the Queen Elizabeth Hall as part of the Southern Songwriters Circle, with other singer/writers like Joe South, Vic Chesnutt, Dan Penn and Allen Toussaint. Along with some stories and old favourites, Guy sang two numbers which we hadn't heard before and which gave a foretaste of what was to come with the next album.

Dublin Blues

The first of the two new songs was *The Cape*, a nicely whimsical bit of homespun philosophy about trusting in what you believe in, again using a universal theme – even if as a boy you never pretended to be Captain Marvel and jumped off a fence with a cape around your neck, you probably knew someone who did (and most likely picked him up and dusted him down afterwards).

He's one of those who knows that life
Is just a leap of faith
Spread your arms and hold your breath
And always trust your cape

The first recording of the song was actually done by Kathy Mattea on her 1994 Walking Away a Winner album, and Guy asked her to do the harmony part when he eventually recorded it himself.

"I like that song," says Guy. "Susanna had the idea, and had started writing it with a friend of hers named Jim Janosky; I can't remember how much of it they had but they asked me if I would help, and that's what came out."

Susanna adds: "Jim came to town, and Garth Brooks' manager at the time suggested he come and write songs with me. I said I'd always wanted to write about a guy jumping off a garage with a cape, so we started writing and ended up with about ten verses to this song. I took it to Guy and he looked at it and said, here's what you do! And we cut it down to what it is now."

The other song was indeed the much darker *Dublin Blues*, a cry of pain set to a memory of an old seafaring folk tune.

When the album, which took its title from that song, finally came out in 1995, again on Asylum, it surpassed even BOATS TO BUILD in the strength of its content – it was arguably the finest collection of Guy Clark songs since OLD NO.1. Half of the songs on an album, for the first time in twelve years, were solely Guy's, and the other five had his fingerprints all over them. *Dublin Blues* itself opened the album with a blast of laid-bare emotion:

I wish I was in Austin in the Chili Parlor Bar
Drinking mad dog margaritas and not carin' where you are
But here I sit in Dublin just rollin' cigarettes
Holdin' back and chokin' back the shakes with every breath

Like most of Guy's songs, there is an element of actuality in *Dublin Blues* – there was a time on a European tour when Susanna went off with a friend to Italy, leaving Guy in Dublin. From the writing point of view, partly because he feels it gets closer than usual to Townes

Chili Parlor Bar, Austin
(Randy Jensen)

Van Zandt's way of writing, it's the one Guy rates most highly among his more recent work:

"*Dublin Blues* is my favourite, because it's more of an impressionist painting, you know. Like Robert [Earl Keen] was describing, many of my songs are stories and they have a beginning and end, and it's kind of getting away from that, which I like. It's just a nice, emotional, good piece of songwriting. It works on a lot of levels.

"And it has a beautiful melody – *Handsome Molly*, which was always one of my favourite traditional songs, and I always swore I would steal that melody before I died! It's the folk process! That first line, that's another line that I actually wrote down and carried for years and years: 'I wish I was in Austin, in the Chili Parlor bar, drinking mad dog margaritas and not caring where you are.' And I tried to get several people to help, tried to get Rodney to write it with me, tried to get Verlon, and they all just looked at me and said, no, no, you have to write that by yourself!"

We had commented ourselves on the use of part of the old tune in *Dublin Blues*, and hearing Guy talking about it brought to mind other artful references which find their way into some of his songs: the way the opening line of the first – but no other – verse of *Desperados Waiting For a Train* ('I'd play the Red River Valley') is actually sung to the old *Red River Valley* melody; the echoes of car horns in the guitar line of *LA Freeway*; and the cajun three-step ending to *South Coast of Texas*.

Nanci Griffith sings harmony on the chorus of *Dublin Blues*, and acoustic guitar and penny whistle is provided by a musician who appears for the first time on one of Guy's albums. Miles Wilkinson tells how Darrell Scott came into the picture:

"We were talking about making the next record, and Guy said, okay, we want to add an element, what's it gonna be? So he started talking about bringing in the Whites – Buck White and his two daughters, one of the White daughters married Ricky Skaggs I believe. Buck plays piano, and Guy was talking about bringing him in and just having another sort of rhythm element.

"That sounded interesting to me, but one night anyway we went to a club in town to see Verlon Thompson and his wife play, and of course Guy's a big fan and supporter of Verlon, they've written together a whole lot and Verlon had always played with him on the record – so we went and Verlon and Suzi [Ragsdale, Thompson's wife] were playing in a round situation and they had another guy with them, a fellow that we had met who had recently signed with EMI Publishing, which is where we all ended up by the way – there was another buyout and we all ended up in EMI – this guy's name was Darrell Scott.

"I had met Darrell several times, I had worked with him in the studio already doing publishing work, and thought he was one of the greatest talents I had ever run across, and we were all down there in the club watching them, and Guy, in the break in the first set, he leans over to me and says, that is the single greatest acoustic rhythm guitar player I have ever heard in my life! We gotta have this person on our record. Forget the Buck White thing, this is something really new.

"And I remember being so really amazed because of all the incredible talent Darrell Scott had, the one thing I had sort of never even noticed before was his rhythm guitar playing. Because he is probably the single greatest musician I've ever met in my life, he plays like twenty instruments, every one of them as good as anything else. Great singer/songwriter, too. So I just hadn't noticed that, but in the next set I really paid attention, and I just agreed with Guy about this person; we can use him.

"So we added Darrell Scott to the DUBLIN BLUES record, and Darrell definitely brought in a new sensibility, it's like he took the sound and the music to the next level. And there's a definite difference between that and the previous album with the addition of Darrell. They're both good, it's just that each one has a flavour, and basically I'm explaining to you the reason why these albums have different flavours."

Darrell Scott's first introduction to a Guy Clark song was while he was studying at college, and his girlfriend Sherri (now his wife) made a deal with him that she would make him a quilt if he would teach her guitar! The song she wanted to learn was *LA Freeway*:

"I just heard it on the record she was playing and picked it up from that. I reckon that was the first time I put together like, this is Guy Clark, this is the guy I've heard about for a long time, I just never really listened to his music – that was back in about '83.

"My first reaction on hearing it was that it was very literate. At the time I was going to school, getting an English degree, so I was kinda tuned, my antennas were up, for just great writing, whether it came from short stories or poetry, or songs especially. And it was just like, well this is great, and then I delved further into OLD NO.1, and there it all was.

"Years before that I had been playing music, and I was in a period in my life where I kinda wanted to get away from music. I actually went to college for four and a half years, and I wasn't eighteen, I was like 25, and so I was going to college and putting music on the back burner, to tell you the truth. What I was really focussing on was just kinda getting a general education, but specifically poetry, short stories; I was getting into the, I don't know, the *word*, the stories of things and leaving music behind. I was really studying and writing a lot of poetry."

In a similar way to Guy himself, Darrell says that for the most part his writing is governed by what happens in his life, but makes a point of crediting Guy for inspiration in the practice of songwriting:

"It's the stories and the quality of the songs, just from beginning to end, the opening lines to the end, just how tight they are and how they just stand up as pieces of work. To me, Guy's one of those who provide the mark; you don't often achieve it, but that doesn't mean your mark gets any lower, and he's one of the marks."

After Darrell graduated, he decided to try and take his new angle on poetry and literature back into music, and through an unlikely set of circumstances ended up with a song publishing contract:

"I was going to school in London for a semester, and a guy I met over there, also on an exchange programme, from the US, knew a family pretty big in the music industry in New York. Anyway, this guy ran EMI Publishing which is where Guy wrote, so it was easy to get a tape to those guys and they liked it and signed me to a publishing and record deal. And part of the development of the record deal was just getting more songs together, so they sent me down to Nashville from Boston, and that's the first time I actually met Guy. They sent me down here to write with him and a couple of other people.

"At the time EMI Publishing was a house, where right now they've incorporated everything all in Music Row, but Music Row used to be a bunch of houses, and Guy had an office at the top of this house at EMI that overlooked the street. He had his books in there, and his saws, and hammers, a bit like his den now, because that's how he used it, he wrote up there. So I went up to the top of the stairs and there he was, and we talked and played a little bit and maybe an hour or two later wrote a song.

"I had some stuff I'd been working on so I threw some of that out to him, he wanted to jump on one of them, and we kind of did it. And then I saw him like about two weeks later up in Boston, he was doing a show up there, a solo thing, and got to see him then, and then when I moved down here I played on a demo of his, and then after that I just started playing on his last two records after that as a player."

The other musicians on the album are basically the same as on BOATS TO BUILD: the nucleus of Travis Clark on bass, Verlon Thompson on second guitar and harmony vocals, and Kenny Malone on drums and percussion; Darrell explains some of the technical aspects of having three acoustic guitars in the band:

"I got added to that team after BOATS TO BUILD. Partly as a guitarist – there are some times, like on DUBLIN BLUES or whatever, where me and Verlon and Guy all are going to play guitar – and sometimes on mandolin or Dobro. The way we decide that, it's largely just like what anyone thinks, it's a real open forum, no-one's kinda telling anybody what to do, it's real organic.

"But also, I can tell you this, that the first day of the sessions of the DUBLIN BLUES album, I went in knowing Guy's gonna be playing guitar, Verlon's gonna be playing guitar and in some cases I will be too, actually in a lot of cases. So I went in needing to find a space that would complement and work with three guitars: Guy in the centre and me and Verlon off to either side. One of the first things I did was, I had this old guitar that never sounded any good for the regular tunes, and I tuned it down so I actually got sort of a low string guitar – I found that was one of the things I could do so it didn't just sound like a guitar army, just to be in a different space sonically.

"I played that on *Baby Took a Limo*, and *Dublin Blues* has something like that on it, and the things that sound like I'm playing an open

Mainstage, Edmonton Festival 1994
(Edmonton Festival archive)

tuning, but they're just low tuned. It happened several other times too, I would basically track with the guitars so there'd be three guitars going. But that was part of the experiment on my part of just trying to find a place where the guitar could fit in there with what was already great, as it was with BOATS TO BUILD and OLD FRIENDS.

"It could have been disastrous, but Verlon and I, we've played a lot together, and we're also just giant ears, we both listen, we're both footed in the songs, foremost. If I had to say anything to playing with Guy Clark it would be that I'm a slave to the song and there's no better songs out there than Guy's. And if you sit there as a musician and react to those songs and those lyrics, it just doesn't get any better, and I've played on a lot of great songs."

In spite of the importance that the principal characters attach to the organic feel of the recording, it wouldn't be a Guy Clark studio album without a few welcome guests, like Jonathan Yudkin on violin and Sam Bush on mandolin, to add their little bits of magic to the sound. And as well as Kathy Mattea and Nanci, Rodney Crowell and

Emmylou each sing harmony on one number.

Rodney, appropriately, also plays an acoustic guitar solo – and his old partner Donivan Cowart sings harmony – on *Black Diamond Strings*, a waltz time tribute to the whole Crowell clan:

Let Rodney sit in, hell, he's goin' on nine
His fingers are bleedin' but he's keepin' good time

Guy: "We were living in that house in East Nashville. Rodney and Donivan Cowart, who's his long time pal, engineer, they were playing together and singing as a duet. I met them somewhere and they came over to the house and just started hanging out, and it grew throughout the years.

"I met his parents later, a few years later. And his dad was a player, you know, had a band, they played every weekend in what they call an ice house. It's like, in Texas they have drive-in markets, but with big sliding overhead doors that they open to let a breeze through because of the heat. And usually on Friday and Saturday nights there would be music – a little band would play. And Rodney did that every weekend with his dad, I think when he was about eleven or something. Started playing drums, and whoever didn't show up, that's what he would play – guitar, bass.

"A good way to learn, yeah, he knows – he has an incredible encyclopaedic memory of music in his head. Songs, every country song. He said he had a band one time in high school and could play every Beatles song that had been released!"

We asked Rodney if he liked the song, and were taken aback by the strength of his reaction: "Oh man, I *love* that song! That song's as much about my mother as it is about my father, that's just a beautiful thing, you know, Guy calls it a love song. I mean I haven't ever been able to express really how moved I've been by that song."

Rodney is the co-writer of *Stuff That Works*, which, as we've said before, is one of the definitive songs of the whole Guy Clark oeuvre: "That's one of my favourite songs that Guy and I wrote. I was kinda down, thinking about hanging myself because I'd been on the road for a couple of years and things had kind of fallen apart for me. So we made some time, and Guy came over and he just said, I got this idea, let's write a song about stuff! And we started hacking away on it, and he went home and came back and I had written a bunch of stuff on my own to go with it.

"And this is the great thing about Guy, the editor that he is: I thought it was pretty good, and he went through it and went no, no, no, threw it all out, and I thought, this is really good stuff and he's throwing it away, and you know what, he was right! And that's when it turned the corner and we started coming up with the stuff that the song became, and I love that song, it is my favourite that we wrote together."

Guy adds: "I had started that song, and had a lot of it written, but it was waltz time and it didn't have a chorus, and I asked Rodney to try and help me make it a song. And he did! It's about stuff needing to be used. Not trophies, tools. It's like people who collect guitars and never take them out of the house. You can't play this, this is too precious. Well, fuck it! Why would you have it! I mean, that's just me, you know. I don't like stuff that's too precious to play. So what? That's what that song's about."

Shut Up and Talk to Me is a fun song, written with Susanna and Keith Sykes. "That's just a goofy song. Actually, it's a woman's song, and it's meant for a woman to do, but it was just so much fun, I just couldn't, you know, resist it. That one, we only recorded it twice or something, the basic tracks until I got the vocal, in one or two takes, and I'd never really played that song, or didn't really know it, so the breaks got kinda long. And it was like, well Kenny [Malone, the percussionist] hadn't got to play a solo on this record, so Kenny, why don't you play something here, and it just kinda evolved into this… he's a marvellous guy, we both moved to Nashville about the same time some 25 years ago, and he had just gotten out of the Navy, he was 20 years in the Navy – he retired from it 25 years ago – and played in a Navy band, played marimbas, so it's not only percussion, it's musical too, I mean he reads, he's not just a drummer, he's just like incredible to work with, amazing."

Hank Williams Said it Best is, like *Too Much* on the previous album, what Guy calls a laundry list song, with the verses written to the same repeating structure as Butch Hancock's *Tell Me What You Know*.

"*Too Much* is cool," says Guy. "I would love to learn it, but I'm just too lazy. *Hank Williams Said it Best* is one I would edit, though.

When I wrote that, I had all these verses, verse after verse after verse and was trying to decide what to leave out, and Susanna listened to a rough demo of it and she said, man if you leave any of that out I'm divorcing you! You gotta put it all in, don't edit, don't edit!

"And now I wish I had, because I could edit that song down to, like, three verses, and have it be a really good, tight song. And I still might do that. Actually I wouldn't do it by verse, I'd do it by line, because they're all entertaining. There's no real thread. Matter of fact, that's the way I'll write sometimes. With those kind of songs I'll have all these couplets and just strip them up with a knife, move them back and forth, finally get something and tape it together!"

Tryin' to Try is almost a throwaway love song except for the delightfully off the wall verses:

I threw a rock through your window
Just to let you know I love you
Just to let you know I care and I ain't scared
To have you see how I feel

Baby Took a Limo to Memphis is the bluesy story of Susanna's trip to see Keith Sykes, which she talks about later in the book; *Hanging Your Life on the Wall* has a nice joint vocal with Jack Elliott; and lastly (but hardly least) *The Randall Knife* is, of course, the definitive reading of the song first heard on BETTER DAYS.

Keepers

Word that Guy Clark was to bring out a live album in 1997 filtered out through various web sites and Internet newsgroups, and the venue for the recording – the Douglas Corner Café in Nashville on Hallowe'en night, 1996 – was filled with people who had got advance warning it was to take place there. But one surprising aspect of the album was that it would not be coming out on Asylum Records. Miles Wilkinson explains why Guy changed labels:

"I think that was political more than anything else. Guy was originally signed to Asylum because Kyle Lehning was put in charge of the label, which had been dead for many years but got reactivated in Nashville. Kyle had been producing Randy Travis, and I think he did some of the early Dirt Band stuff too. So he took a look at the history of Asylum Records and realised that it was a very unique label as a singer-songwriter label, and that there was an integrity there of quality songs and quality artists, not just to make money. And he wanted to make a statement that he intended to carry on the tradition of Asylum Records, of its past history, and even though clearly they wanted to activate it so they could try to become a mainstream country label, he wanted to let people know that he wasn't going to lose the historical thread either.

"So Guy was the first signing, which was a big surprise to people in Nashville at that time, and he did two records for Guy. The problem was, by the time we finished our second record – I guess Asylum had been active here in Nashville for a couple of years – they basically had had no hits on anybody, and they were struggling terribly.

"Well, I think the powers that be just decided that after we did two albums and didn't sell very many records that it was time to make a change, and unfortunately in that process Guy got lost in the cracks! And it wasn't long after that that Kyle started signing successful country albums and Asylum really took off, you know, with financial success. And he kind of also made the statement, well, I've got two Guy Clark records in the can, and they're on the label and they'll always be there, so…

"Plus I think they realised that Guy just wasn't wanting to be the type of person that was going to go out and do the star thing – Guy is just going to be Guy and that's all there is to it, you know, he's going to write his songs, write great songs and go out and perform, and he's not interested in doing coliseums, doing all that real hard, tough, promo and radio work and stuff. You know, Guy's happy with his life.

"So all those things I think contributed. An interesting thing, though, as a result of those three records we made, suddenly Guy had all kinds of people trying to sign him – Oh Boy Records; I know Warners in Nashville was looking at him; of course, every small label in the business was trying – and Guy talked to a lot of people and in fact took an incredibly long period of time making his mind up.

"During that period Guy and I sat down and started talking about what this next album was going to be. And basically he said, okay well, you know how you and I have always talked about someday doing a record where we would do all the old tunes in the new way, he said I think the time's come, so now we're going to get ready and plan to make the record we always talked about making, and everything else was sort of getting ready to make that record. And Guy comes up with this idea, you know what, I think maybe in order to make it a little different and to also be incredibly honest about this stuff, we should do a live record. So that was his idea. And we started planning that project, and somewhere in the middle of that he decided to go back to Sugar Hill Records and sign the deal with them."

Guy adds: "I always wanted to do a live album. I originally picked 25 songs to do. But it got unwieldy in that the cost of recording and mixing 25 songs was considerable, twice as much in fact, coupled with the fact that the record company would have had to pay the publishing royalties on all of those 25 songs. I don't think it's fair for record companies to ask artists or writers to let them use their song for a reduced rate. There's a statutory rate, which it should be, right.

"So I'm in the middle of that, because I'm also the artist – I want to do all these songs – but I don't want to pay for them – well shit, I wrote them! – you know, that's me, saying all that! So anyway, that was a compromise that was mainly economic, just like, well I can't afford to do this – *do this* – okay. But I can do a whole other album, just like that. And we have them, all rehearsed. Yeah, when I started rehearsing to do that, we did, like 24, 25 songs."

Miles continues the story of the making of KEEPERS:

"Initially I thought, the element that's new and fresh about this fourth record will be the live thing, but then we made a further decision to add musically one more element, and that was Suzi Ragsdale. She had been playing an awful lot with Verlon and with Darrell, and in fact Verlon and Suzi had been doing a duet thing for a number of years, they did a couple of records of their own, and also Guy had quite a number of performances, special performances with not only Travis, but with Verlon and Suzi and Darrell. So Suzi had already been doing quite a few of the live shows and she'd been playing accordion, and it had been working out real nice, so Guy said, I want to have Suzi there also.

"So we planned the band for the live record, which would be Travis on bass, Verlon on second guitar, Darrell on third guitar and anything else he felt like playing! And of course drums for the record, which Guy never does live, our only choice was Kenny because Kenny is the most unique drummer on the planet – and then we added the new element which is Suzi playing accordion. Suzi had sung some harmonies on previous records, but this was really making her part of the band, so that was the new element.

"And then we recorded live – starting with Hallowe'en we recorded four nights and edited the best takes together, and something that was virtually unheard of on a live record – we did not overdub anything, which was the only way we could do it with Guy. Now I want to be totally honest about that – I had a lot of trouble with the recording facility we hired and we ended up with some technical problems where the first night one of Verlon's instrument never got on tape, in fact the first night we never got any kick drum on tape! It's a long story, but we ended up doing a very few small overdubs just to replace things that for some reason didn't get on there or got on with some bad noises or distortion.

"In fact there was only one song where we really had to completely re-record one instrument, and that was one of Verlon's slide parts. But it was never because the playing wasn't right, or we were trying to improve something, you know, from that point of view, it was once I decided this was a problem, we didn't have any choice. So that was a remarkable album – so many of these live albums they go in and redo all the vocals, but not in this case. So we did that, made those technical fixes, mixed it and bang, it was out, and Sugar Hill released it.

"I guess the only other noteworthy thing to say was between the recording and the mastering of that record is when Townes died, and I think Townes had been dead only a couple of weeks when we did the mastering. And that was a very intense time with Guy during the mastering process, it was a very emotional time."

The material on KEEPERS is largely older songs from Guy's repertoire, plus two new numbers, *A Little of Both* by Guy and Verlon Thompson and *Out in the Parking Lot*, co-written with Darrell Scott, which Guy says is one of the songs he currently plays that he finds has universal recognition: "I've played that in Australia and other places, everybody knows what that song is about!"

According to Darrell, the inspiration for the rhythmic feel of *Parking Lot* came from an unlikely source, Bruce Springsteen:

"We wrote that song out of that second get together we had. Guy had just about all of those lyrics, he had the bulk of that song, and had for, it sounded like it was a couple of years. He tried it every way, with different folk, tried to find a way to do those lyrics – and the same with me, we tried, I don't think I've ever worked so hard on a song in my life. Actually I'm certain of it, I tend to give up before that!

"We worked for days on that, at first it was dressing those words up in different ways, we tried country shuffle, we tried honky tonk stuff, we did it about the bar scene, different things like that. Then at one point Guy said, well how would Springsteen do this? We had been talking about *Racing in the Street* while we were hanging out those few days there, that's a classic, that's a great song.

"We also listened to other songs – that's part of what writing with Guy is, you know, he may play a great old Bob Dylan song or a great Townes song, you know what I mean, it's not just writing, it's turning you on to a bunch of stuff. But anyway, that kind of crystallised for me when he said, well how would Springsteen do this, and in my own way that helped me to find a melody and chords and vibe for it, the way we do that now. So we wrote a few more words, you know, a verse here, a chorus there, whatever, and after several days we had the song. We were glad to see that one come down the pipe!"

You won't find many live albums with as warm a feel to them as KEEPERS. Guy's dry humour comes through in the brief song introductions, and everyone seems to be having a real good time. It probably surprised everyone concerned when it was nominated in the 'best contemporary folk album' category in the 1998 Grammy Awards, but it was no more than it deserved.

Guy & Travis on stage, Crazy Horse Steakhouse, Santa Ana, c.1996
(Toni Marteney)

Interlude: SUSANNA CLARK

SUSANNA Clark is herself a Texan. She was born in Atlanta, in the east of the state; her mother decided on the name because, as she said, if it's good enough for Shakespeare's daughter, it's good enough for mine! Susanna is a beautiful lady in early middle age, with flowing silver-grey hair that, like Emmylou Harris, she refuses to colour. She had been unwell for some time when we met her, but she came out of her bedroom and introduced herself with an innate graciousness, and showed us round the large living space of their house.

On a table in the middle of the lounge was a cartoon clay model of Guy and the group during the recording of KEEPERS at the Douglas Corner Café, crafted by Susie Monick, and on the wall above the fireplace was Susanna's original painting of the blue denim shirt that graces the cover of the first Guy Clark album, OLD NO. 1. Her original of Willie Nelson's STARDUST cover hangs on another wall. It was a surprise not to see the 'Quarter Moon' painting from Emmylou's fourth album, but she said she gave the painting to Emmylou some years ago.

We spoke to Susanna first in Guy's workshop downstairs. It was one of the few bad days we had in Nashville in an unusually warm and humid early April. As the sky rumbled and rain lashed down through the trees on the hill outside the window, and Guy worked on the Spanish guitar he was making at the bench, Susanna smoked her long, thin cigarettes and talked of their early life together in Houston and Nashville.

"How did you and Guy meet, Susanna?"

"I first saw him once, briefly, some thirty years ago, when I lived with my sister in an apartment in Oklahoma City. Guy and Townes were there on tour – Guy was a friend of my sister – and I walked into my living room, and here sat these two skinny, really grubby looking guys! They both had hair down to the middle of their backs, and I walked in and introduced myself, and the first thing I ever said to Guy was, 'Would you like a vitamin pill?' I was concerned about these boys!

"I was painting at the time and I had the easel set up in my living room. I was having trouble with the foreground – making it come forward, you know, and I was sitting there saying, 'What do I do about this,' and Guy said, '*You* know what to do,' and I thought, well, I can't drop my artistic hankie in front of him – that doesn't work!

"Guy got up and said a few things about the painting and I thought, that's wonderful, he knows what to do with paint; I was very attracted to the way he dealt with this painting. He was as serious about art as I was."

"Do you remember that meeting, Guy?" asked Nick.

"Sure do."

"The attraction was mutual?"

"Oh, of course. I just thought she was beautiful, smart. Had vitamins!"

"Which sounds like a bit of a plus at the time," said Nick.

Guy grinned. "Anything in pill form…"

Susanna laughed and carried on. "Then a few months later my sister died – she was 26 – and I called him to tell him. He told me that the very same week he was on his way to his home town, Monahans, for the funeral of the man that was most dear to him, Jack Prigg, the man Guy wrote *Desperados Waiting For a Train* about. He was grieving quite a bit about that, and then this phone call I'm sure really threw him.

"Well, I was completely devastated by my sister's death – it was quite sudden – and so after he went to Monahans he came to Oklahoma City. Someone said we were 'united in grief', which I think was true. We were both really broken, and were very consoling to each other. He went back to Houston and we talked on the phone – you get to know each other very well and very quickly when you each lose a loved one like that, and very deeply, and of course he knew my sister as well. We talked on the phone every day for a long time. He asked me to move down there, and I wanted to. I moved to Houston to be with him. And that's what happened."

"You had been painting for a while?"

"Yes, I had. I was oil-painting, and was also teaching art at the Oklahoma City Science & Arts Foundation. I had done the graphic images at the Oklahoma City Zoo. I had a degree in psychology and philosophy, but I really wanted to paint. I was selling a few at that point, and teaching painting."

"So when did you move to Houston?"

"July 4th. He came up to get me, and we moved in."

Guy and Susanna, Nashville, c.1976 (Jim McGuire)

Guy growled from the bench, "One of our anniversaries. When's the other one, Susanna?"

"January 14th. He thinks I forget them all the time! He gives me these wonderful, beautiful, lovely presents and I've forgotten. The last one, he surprised me. We were having lunch with Jack Elliott and Wayland Holyfield and Roy Rogers, who produced Ramblin' Jack and, oh, a lot of people, and suddenly a dozen roses arrived and beautiful engraved silver champagne glasses – he'd thought about it a long time – and I said, 'What is all this for?' and he said, 'It's our anniversary,' and I'd forgotten any of that, but it arrived at lunch. So the whole table knew I'd forgotten!"

Guy added, "And then there was my birthday… it's not that she has a bad memory, it's just – short. Susanna tells me she could hide her own Easter Eggs."

"And Guy tells me I'm a goose in magicland… living on higher planes…"

Susanna left the room for a moment to put on a more comfortable robe. Guy continued planing a piece of wood, occasionally grunting with satisfaction or irritation. When she returned we asked about the music she was into at that time.

"At that time I was listening to Bob Dylan every day, over and over again, constantly. I had taken a few guitar lessons when I was in high school, and I had written poetry all my life, but until I met Guy I didn't realise you could put them together! When I moved to Houston, it was a different culture for me. I hadn't associated with hippies at all and I moved into a big house that was surrounded by hippies hanging out of windows. I thought, what have I gotten myself into? But I started painting in Houston, and painted a lot and began to sell some. It was a pretty terrible adjustment period; my sister had just died and I was now living in a city where I knew no-one.

"At that point Guy was still the art director of a television station, and I painted all day. I was quite alone – Guy was at work all day long – and I was feeling quite isolated. No-one had really been kind to me, it didn't feel as if I fitted in very well. One day we were at someone's house; there were quite a few people there I didn't know, but I had met Townes a couple of times, and Townes came up to me at this party and put his arms around me and very sincerely looked me in the eye and gave me a big hug and said, 'If Guy loves you, I love you.' And for the first time I felt as if somebody meant it, it was so touching to me, and for the first time I felt at home. We started being great friends then."

"It must have been a time of big changes for you."

"There were very dramatic changes, because I came from a different culture in Oklahoma City than the one I moved to in Houston, and I didn't really know the ways of that particular culture. I was quite shocked –"

"But you learned pretty quickly!"

"Oh yes, I learned very quickly. When somebody pulled out marijuana I went, 'Ugh,' and they talked about acid and things like that. But while I was down there, there were a lot of guitar pickers that came over every day and we had a house right in the centre of this community – it was a very big house so it was easy for a lot of people to drop by – so I listened to a lot of good music. Guy played at the Old Quarter on weekends, so I always went to the gigs and loved the music that I was hearing from Townes and from Guy, and from so many other people. Frank Davis was down there playing a lot, and Pete Gorisch."

Nick asked, "What was it about Guy's songs that you liked?"

"Guy hadn't written a lot when I met him, but he wrote one that I loved because it was about me, it had my name in it! *Susanna Let Your Hair Down*, I think that was the name of it."

"Thought that was about you, huh?" said Guy.

Susanna ignored this. "Oh, another one he wrote I loved was called *Step Inside This House*, that was so beautiful. I loved it because it set a mood and also it took pictures of everything, it explained things – you're there when you're listening to Guy's songs. That song has just been cut by Lyle Lovett.

"Lyle called me from LA a few weeks ago and said, 'Susanna, I've just cut *Step Inside This House*, and I want to play it for you right now,' and he played it for me over the phone, the rough mix. He said, 'I want to do it exactly like Guy did it, and you're the only one who knows how he used to do that.' So I listened to it and it was beautiful. He had done a beautiful job on it.

"And then he wanted to play me a couple of Townes' songs that he had done. One was *Flying Shoes*, because, he said, 'You know how this goes.' Well *he* knew, because he does those songs all the time, but he wanted to see if it was right. They were beautiful. He said he was doing a lot of songs by Texas writers, and he tried to stay as faithful to the song and the way it was written as possible. So I said, 'Lyle, you're doing a great job, I'm sure Townes is with you right there, right now,' and he said, 'Well you and Guy are too.' That was so sweet. And he said thank you, and said he'd send me a copy." [A few weeks later Susanna phoned and said they had just received copies of the CD, which Lyle named STEP INSIDE THIS HOUSE after Guy's song.]

"So there we were in Houston, and I loved to listen, so I started to try and fool around with the guitar again, just a little, simply because there were so many people there doing it all the time, and I started relearning how to play, and write a little bit. Then it finally dawned on me that Guy wasn't happy. I asked Guy what he wanted to do with his life, and he said, 'I want to do music,' and I said, 'Well, you're at a television station as an artist, and if you really want to do music then quit your job.'

"He said, 'What! no woman has ever told me to quit a job before!' So I said, 'No producer is going to come knocking on your door in hippieville in Houston – quit your job and let's go to someplace that you think they'll listen.' So I sold my car and some paintings and we packed everything we could pack – and threw away everything we couldn't – into a Volkswagen van and drove to Los Angeles. Guy knew one person in LA, that's why we decided to go there, and I was working on The Shirt [the OLD NO.1 cover painting] at the time. We found a little bitty bitty place in Long Beach, it was not far from the Dobro factory where Guy got a job. We made it through, but it was really rough. I lost weight! We didn't even have a phone. But it was still fun."

"When Guy got the songwriting deal, how did things change for you?"

"We decided to pack up and go to Nashville. We found a *leeetle* house in East Nashville –"

Guy pointed to one of the black and white photos lying on the table in front of us. "That house."

" – on Chapel Street. Guy got fifty dollars a week. Then we decided to get married on – on –"

"What day was it?" asked Guy.

Susanna laughed again. "He loves to tease me about that! I remember them a *lot*! As a matter of fact I remembered a lot of them at first and he didn't, and I just gave up, and now all of a sudden he's giving me these great gifts hoping I'll remember! I remembered all these things at first and he didn't remember anything for ten years, so I said hey, to hell with it, now I'm getting silver things and flowers all the time."

Nick said, "That's nice..."

"Yeah, it's very nice, I'm glad he reacted that way! We found that place, and out of that fifty dollars, we also had to send child support back to Guy's ex-wife, so we decided to get married and we got married on Mickey Newbury's houseboat.

"We got on the houseboat and went down the river to a small town. Guy called Townes – he was in New York – to come down and be his best man at the wedding. So Mickey Newbury and his wife Susan, Townes and Guy and I got on this houseboat and went for a couple of hours down the river, got off the houseboat and got married by a judge, then got back on the houseboat and navigated our way back to Nashville.

"Well, Townes came down to be the best man at our wedding and he stayed for eight months! Which was all right, because he was cutting a record, the first one that Jack Clement produced. Townes had no money, so in that little house the three of us stayed."

"That was OK for you, newly married, with Townes there?"

"Oh, of course! Well, I was kinda baffled at first, but then I realised that Guy – and Townes – well, he had the other bedroom in the house, it was my art studio."

At this point, Susanna's back started troubling her, so we went upstairs to her bedroom to continue the conversation. Susanna sat propped up on the bed with pillows, and carried on smoking, stubbing each cigarette out before it was half-finished. The storm had grown worse, and the thunder and lightning occasionally derailed her train of thought, but the room was lit up by the pleasure she took in relating these memories of the three of them, Guy, Susanna and Townes, in their prime. At several points she became more and more animated, and her almost latin gestures conveyed far more than mere words on the page can. We just sat back in chairs by the bed and listened...

"We'd go to record company parties and stuff our jackets with the hors d'oeuvres. We would go to any free party there was, and then Townes and Guy and I had a way of stealing the whisky and all the booze we could. We would go outside, somebody would slip it under a jacket and somebody would go and put it under a lamppost and by the time we left the party we had a lot underneath that lamppost! That was fun."

"Who looked after the money, Susanna?"

"Nobody took care of it, we just somehow slid by, it didn't matter. One sweet man – he was the father of one of the secretaries at Guy's publishing company – would come by and give us toilet paper and frozen pizzas every Friday! And a lot of people invited us to dinner, and we managed somehow. And with Townes and Guy playing all the time, there were so many people coming to the house. Guy started writing beautiful things, he wrote *Let Him Roll* there.

"But it was a lot of fun, and the strangeness in all three of us came out then. Once Guy spent a great deal of time underneath the kitchen table! We sat around this table all the time, and Guy would get under it and people would come in, they would say, 'How're you doing down there, Guy?' and Guy would say, 'fine!'

"And then there was the time Guy got furious at both of us – Townes loved to tell this story, but he's not here now, so I have to tell it for him – we were laughing too much about something, making fun of him, I've forgotten what it was but he got very angry at both of us and hammered himself in the bedroom! All of a sudden we heard this BAM! BAM! BAM! He got a long nail and hammered himself in and stayed in there. He was not speaking to us, and Townes and I would say, 'Guy, come on out now, what is it?', and we'd sit out there and say, 'What do we do now?'

"The door, thank goodness, had an opening at the bottom and we'd slide notes under it to him – *all will be better tomorrow!* – for whatever it was, I really don't know why he did that. I guess we were being pretty awful, but we loved to laugh. He was there all day. I was worried about his being hungry so we flattened down a

Susanna with Charlie Bundy (Guy & Susanna Clark collection)

tunafish sandwich and stuck it under the door!

"And one time Townes and Guy got very very sick. It was the 'flu or something, and I was their only lifeline. I brought them cough syrup and made soup for them and things like that. But I was so excited to have the house all to myself, and I could paint again. There were usually these pickers there all the time, sometimes I'd find bodies under the couch the next morning! And I painted a painting, it's called The Bouncing Apple – it's in there in the kitchen now. There's this apple bouncing along, and I was so happy, I had the place to myself and there were these two boys moaning in there, and I was absolutely thrilled that they were down for a few days! But I did nurse them back to health. I'll show you the painting later."

"So by this time there was about $100 a week coming in, but it still wasn't that much when all the outgoings for the three of us was taken into account. As a matter of fact, for a long time our staple diet was Bean Surprise – the surprise was whether there were hot dogs or only beans in it! It got so bad at one time that we were reduced to flipping our last quarter to decide whether to get a coke or a popsicle!

"Then out of the blue Townes sold a song, and received a cheque for $500! Well! You can imagine – it was *un*believable! That was a *huge* sum of money to us at that time. And Townes was so sweet and so wonderful, the first thing he said was – you know, Townes was drinking quite a bit then – but instead of racing down to the liquor store like he would have done, or instead of blowing it, the first thing he said was, 'Alright everybody, the first thing we're going to do is buy Susanna' – I was out of white paint for painting, and I had been for months, I couldn't afford it – he said, 'We're going to the art store and buy Susanna some white paint.'

"I was amazed at the kindness and sweetness of that man. So we went to the art store like three of the proudest people in the world, and we walked up to the counter, and said, I *will* have some Permalba White please, and the clerk said, large or small? and Townes said LARGE! It was so sweet. That was the priority with the three of us, art of any kind."

"And I bet you didn't eat Bean Surprise that week!"

"No, we didn't! We were pretty crazy, and that $500 was gone in a week – we just went berserk. But that's alright, because I think Townes bought a used fiddle, and there was some girl – he called the Old Quarter in Houston, and to the first girl that answered the phone, he said, 'Would you like to come to Nashville?' So he bought her a plane ticket to Nashville, and she came, and he didn't even know her last name, so he put the ticket under his name, Mrs Van Zandt, and when she got here she said, 'Do you think that means Townes wants to marry me?!'" Susanna dissolved into fits of giggles at the thought. "It was *so* funny."

"So were they performing at this time?" asked Nick.

"Oh yes. Townes was recording at the time and Townes and Guy would go to a place called Bishop's Pub and play, and they would go to the Exit/In, that's when the Exit/In was a folk club, we hung around there a lot. Oh yeah, they played a lot of places – for free, or for drinks or whatever – we'd go to a lot of places that they'd play."

"And did you perform with them?"

"Oh no, I never perform, I'm just not an entertainer. I like to write and so forth, but you know I always say microphones eat their young, I can't possibly do that. I have severe anxiety in front of a crowd of people. Of course, I sang in front of them as I was writing songs."

"How many have you written?"

"Gee, I don't know, I have three different catalogs with different publishing companies, I don't know how many. Someone made for me a tape of all the ones that were recorded by other people, but there are some new ones since then."

"In England, we usually only get to hear the more popular ones."

"Yeah, I know what you mean. But between Jerry Jeff and Guy and Townes, who were professional songwriters, I finally learned how to write what I wanted to, and play, and I finished a song but I was too frightened to call the publisher. Jerry Jeff and Guy and I had been up all night and we were shooting pool in the morning in this bar, and I finally had enough courage to take this song down to the publisher, and he got it recorded in one day, and it became a number one hit before Townes or Jerry Jeff or Guy had one! They didn't like that!"

"Which one was it?" asked Jeff.

"*I'll Be Your San Antone Rose*, that one."

"That's on LUXURY LINER, isn't it?"

"Yes, but it was recorded first by a girl named Dottsy, and it was the first song she had ever cut, she was trying to be a country singer at the time. And a few weeks later we walked in to the publisher and he said, 'Susanna, you have a number one hit,' and Guy just looked at me and said, 'Bitch!' Here I was, this little fledgling painter, writer, and they were pretty sick! Jerry Jeff said, 'Goddammit, teach her a C chord, look what happens!' And Townes just said, '*What?*' – Townes was very polite. I'm certainly not saying that I write any better than they do, but to have the first stroke of luck was pretty funny!"

"How wonderful!"

"Well, it was, and had I not been exposed to all those people who came through our house – Dave Loggins, David Allan Coe, Skinny Dennis came by – oh, and Rodney Crowell came over a lot, he apprenticed himself to Guy, sort of, but he became a very, very dear friend of mine. So anyway, I had the big bucks now! But by then, Guy had written some wonderful songs, and was about to do OLD NO.1.

"Then Mickey Newbury found us a log cabin on the lake, with a great big fireplace, just a little ways from Mickey, who had a cabin as well. That was where Guy wrote *Shade of All Greens*. I was painting a painting out there that had as many different shades of green in it as I could possibly get, a lot of leaves and so forth, over a stone fence. I'm not sure that's why he wrote that, but both of those things happened at the same time.

"But eventually the man who owned the cabin wanted to move back in it, so we moved right into the middle of town, in an upstairs apartment in an old house. It was right around the corner from Bishop's Pub and a *lot* of people came. I started painting there again. Townes was finally through with his album and was on the road, but he came back and stayed with us quite a bit.

"But I remember one time – Townes used to tell this on stage too – we had a lot of mice up there, a lot of them. There were so many, as a matter of fact, in that old house that Guy and Townes developed this way of getting rid of them. One would sweep the mice into a big paper sack, and they would take this sack down to Bishop's Pub and let all the mice loose on the pool table! And I was going, 'Oh no, Townes!' And they'd scurry to the little holes, and Townes said that every time they sank a ball, Susanna would break into tears! Which I did! They played pool on top of the mice, which was terrible!"

"Rodney and Guy and I had got to be very, very close. Rodney was young and struggling – he was much younger than we were. He had been in town for one week when we met him, and he and his partner Donivan Cowart came up from Texas to become singers – a duet of some sort. Rodney at that point was sleeping on the couch at Richard Dobson's – he was a friend of ours – and so we went over to Richard's house and Rodney was there. In those days Nashville was so beautiful because a lot of people would gather around and we'd pick guitar all day long. It was not like it is now, which is very businesslike, nobody sees anybody. Back then it was, 'Pass the guitar around and sing your latest song,' and if everybody says, *let's kill him*! that means they love it, and it was so much fun.

"Guy was in the kitchen and I was sitting in a little hallway outside the living room, and Rodney came over. He just looked like there were stars twinkling all around him, he was so bright and fresh and such a wonderful kid, and I said, 'Hi!' and he said, 'Hi!' and he sat down and I said, 'Tell you what, I'll play you a song if you play me a song,' and he said, 'That's a deal!' and we were laughing and everything, and so I played a song for him, I've forgotten what I played, but he played one called *There's Glue on My Stool* and I laughed so hard and I just said, 'I like you!' and he said, 'I like you too!' and we became very good buddies, the three of us became great pals.

"Rodney lived across the way, across the park from us, and he was washing dishes in Friday's restaurant. And we had ten dollars we would pass back and forth to go to the movies, and we forgot whose it was, so whoever had it would say, 'Do you want to go to the movies this week – here's the ten dollars.' They'd go to the movies and next week we'd pass it back! It was fun, that was our famous ten dollars, we still remember that."

"They sound really great times."

"The spirit there between us all was so good – nobody cared anything about the way they dressed, looked or anything – it was so conducive to writing and so much fun. Rodney went up and met Emmylou Harris, and she eventually became a part of the group, and she's still one of my dearest friends today.

"Those were great days, fantastic days, there was so much creativity, it was like, I don't know if Guy told you this, but to me it was like living in Paris in the twenties, there were so many brilliant, creative people there, and we were all so united."

Nick said, "As you were talking, I've been reminded of Scott Fitzgerald and the way he spoke about when he lived in Paris –"

"Yeah, that's exactly it. That's when Rodney wrote *Till I Can Gain Control Again* – every time we saw each other, somebody had a new song to share. It was wonderful, there was a lot of support, there wasn't competition in the business part of it or anything like that, it was just a fun support thing, and our house was a gathering place, I'll tell you that."

"So Townes at this time was on the road?"

"Yes, he was on the road, and he was back and forth between Nashville and Texas, and sometimes he'd go to Colorado, but his main location was in Texas at that point, but he was at our house so much it was like he was part of it.

"Then eventually we bought a house, we had enough money to buy a house on the lake, and we lived there for, oh, fifteen years. It was a great old place, windows all around it, two fireplaces. It was only two rooms, only 1500 square feet, and a lot of wonderful songs were written there. Guy and I were writing songs and I was painting. As a matter of fact, I was kinda glad we moved out there, because it was getting too wild living right in town, and I wanted a little peace

Rodney & Susanna, c.1977 (Guy & Susanna Clark collection)

and quiet. But that didn't stop anybody, they came on out anyway, but they had to drive a long way, so the people who really wanted to be there were there, instead of just the people who dropped by for convenience' sake.

"By then Rodney had moved to Los Angeles, but he came out and stayed with us for maybe a week at a time when he visited Nashville. We had got to know Emmylou by then, and she cut *I'll Be Your San Antone Rose*. We had a great big table that Guy had made, and when people came by we gave them a knife and they carved their name and initials and anything they wanted to on the table as we were sitting around on two benches – that table became a work of art. Guy and I went on the road a lot together then."

The storm had died down a little, and the room went quiet for a spell as Susanna lay back and thought about the years in the house by the lake. We waited until she was ready to continue.

"We started doing a lot of drugs, started doing cocaine; things turned kind of cocainish. I'm not sure I should be even saying any of that, but they did for a while – that's when everybody was doing it. It was before we had any idea that it was addictive or anything. It seemed like only musicians were doing it then, you know, it was before everybody had cocaine in their pocket – what do they say about drugs, 'from the classes to the masses' – and back then only the people in studios had it."

"And it was part of the scene."

"Oh yes, it was recreational, it was part of the scene. You couldn't walk anywhere without somebody having it, and nobody knew that it was addictive, nobody. We thought that alcohol was bad, but that was alright!

"Guy had a manager by then, and he was going on the road a lot, and cutting more albums, and I was writing a lot of songs which were being recorded as well. I wrote *I Was Kinda Crazy Then*, and Jerry Jeff cut it, and Jessi Colter cut it, and I wrote *Easy From Now On* with Carlene Carter, and Emmylou cut that. I think it got to be number four or something in the charts, but top five was fine with me. But you can tell with those songs, *Easy From Now On* and stuff like that, that things were getting pretty bad. I was unhappy, and Guy was – we were all getting out of hand."

"How did you pull out of it?"

"I wrote my way out of it. When I was very, very unhappy, I wrote songs about it. I didn't tell anybody things were getting bad between us, I just told the world! I put it on the radio with songs! I didn't tell anybody there were troubles because we had to be Ken and Barbie. At that point, people were thinking we were so happy. Five different couples said we looked so beautiful and wonderful together that they got engaged, because we gave them hope. But little did they know it was quite hard to do, to put on that sort of a front. So nobody understood where these sad songs were coming from, but people kept cutting them, and it was really a release for me.

"So anyway, I put myself on a plane and went to Ridgeway, the place we called dope school, and thank goodness we had enough money to be able to afford it. That was fifteen years ago. And I haven't done cocaine in fifteen years. So I went to this place, and Guy came down on visitors' day, on family day, and then he turned himself in to a recovery place as well.

"And we really turned around, really quickly, because I didn't realise how destructive it was for both of us; drugs can really destroy everything. I came back and things got kinda better, but it was still pretty crazy, and there were a lot of people still doing it – it was getting much more popular. And I had really wanted to do this, to remove myself from that scene and our situation, so eventually I moved to Franklin for about four years.

"Guy and I were still dating, we were still best friends, but I moved as far on the other side of town, to Franklin, as he lived on that side of town, so that I could remove myself from all of the people. I stopped drinking and doing drugs, stopped everything, and got very very healthy. But that doesn't mean that we weren't – let's see, what was it that Paul Newman said about Joanne Woodward, he said, 'Sometimes we're married and sometimes we're not married, but we've never been divorced!' Well, we were not married, but we were not divorced, that's what it was during that time."

"Sounds quite healthy."

"It was! It was the most wonderful thing! It was the healthiest thing because that house was too small for two artists anyway and the things we were doing. I needed my space, he needed his space, and I just moved away to a wonderful little town. I got into therapy, and got better, and he could do whatever he wanted to do. I certainly did what I wanted to do, and I wrote some more songs there – that's when I wrote *Come From the Heart* – and cleaned up, and found out how much trouble, really, I had been getting into, and thank goodness I got out of it. And Townes lived not far from me when I lived in Franklin, and he would come over and see me a lot.

"And that's when I met Richard Leigh, and he and I wrote *Come From the Heart* together – Guy had insisted that we meet – and we wrote a song that Crystal Gayle recorded, called *Whenever it Comes to You*, and one called *Surprise Baby I Can Fly!* – which never did get cut, but Matraca Berg did the demo for me. I had so many people doing demos for me that became stars: Kathy Mattea used to do my demos, Holly Dunn did some for me – that's what they did for a living to support themselves – so these girls all became stars and I had no-one to do my demos for me! But other girls started coming and said, you must be a good luck charm, so they wanted to do them for me!

"I really thrived out there in Franklin because I was getting clean and so forth, and Guy visited me and I visited him, but he was on the road a lot too; it was really healthy for our relationship as well, and we spoke all the time."

"And you didn't have to be Ken and Barbie."

"That's exactly right. And I blossomed... I grew a great deal at that point, I really did, and I had a wonderful time. But as a healing thing, what I did was, I had been wearing Guy's leftover blue jeans and t-shirts that we got at gigs, all that time. So at that point I had made quite a bit of money, and went on wild shopping sprees and got all these designer clothes, I got my hair fou-fou'd, and all buffed and puffed, I bought myself a big old car, I really did a healing trip! I was in therapy three times a week for four years, I did everything to shed all of the mess. And that is when I decided to take a limo to Memphis – it was that trip that Guy wrote the song about – just to really pamper myself, really take care of myself."

"Seemed like the thing to do!" quoted Nick.

"Yes! I was writing a song with Keith Sykes and I was going to fly and I thought I was too sensitive to fly, and so I just got a limo! When the going gets tough, the tough go shopping! And Emmylou and I went shopping together, and we became very close friends because both of us have grey hair and refuse to dye it, and we palled around together."

Susanna at home, c.1980 (Guy & Susanna Clark collection)

"So when did you and Guy get back together?"

"Guy and I had lived apart for about four years, and I had to have a very serious operation. Well, I had the operation and while I recuperated in the hospital I was completely immobile – I wasn't even allowed to be out of bed. So I hired a private nurse and so forth, all kinds of people, to take care of me. I thought Guy was busy at the time, he was supposed to be doing the first Elektra/ Asylum album [BOATS TO BUILD], but somebody told Guy about it, and one day Guy showed up and fired everybody! And he said, 'I'm going to take care of you,' and he slept in the bed next to mine in the hospital. Well, one night I woke up haemorrhaging. The call box next to my bed was broken, and thank God Guy was there – he pulled the covers back and there was blood everywhere – Guy really saved my life. The doctors and nurses walked in, and one doctor looked up and said, 'I'll have to ask you to leave the room,' and Guy just stood there, he leaned against the door and said, 'I ain't goin' nowhere!' It was so moving.

"And so we went back to the house, and Guy slept on the couch for weeks looking after me, while he was supposed to be doing this album. If there was anything I wanted, a desire for chocolate-covered lobster, anything, he would get it for me. And he wouldn't let any of the visitors see me for more than fifteen minutes at a time, so as not to tire me out. A side of him came out at that time that was absolutely wonderful.

"And when Guy had to do a gig, Townes came down on his motorcycle and took care of me. He'd sit with me and sing songs to me all the time, and make me scrambled eggs – and his wife said, 'Scrambled eggs? I had no idea he could cook!' Nobody believed these two wild creatures could take care of a sick woman, but they did, and Guy was so wonderful, it was during this time that I fell in love with him all over again."

"And he was still supposed to be doing the album?"

"Oh yes, but he was determined to see I was alright first. I never dreamed he would tell Asylum to wait until I was well, but he did – the executives were screaming about missing deadlines and so forth, but he stuck it out. And when I was well again, we were still theoretically living apart, but Guy kept coming back and back, and spent so much time each time he came back, that finally he never left. And he sort of suggested we move back in together properly, and I said, 'Only if you have one floor and I'll have the other, and you can have all your crazy friends around to watch football or whatever, and I can have my own space,' and we agreed on this, and that was some four, five years ago."

Susanna seemed to be getting tired by now, the story was pretty much up to date, and the recorder had run out of tape, so we said we'd think about packing up and getting out of their hair. Susanna gave each of us a tape of her recorded songs, and wrote a little message on the front, but before we said goodbye and left, she said something that the last couple of hours' conversation had obviously brought very much to the forefront of her thoughts.

"Until he died last year, Townes and I talked on the phone every single morning at 8.30, we talked about everything. It was wonderful, we got very close, and he said that a best man should take his duties seriously, especially when it came to helping with a husband and wife's problems. I wrote something for myself that Rodney convinced me to read at the funeral. I agreed because no-one knew this side of Townes, this relationship between a man and a woman which was not sexual, but could be so close for so many years, with so much love. Would you like to hear it?"

We said, with a little trepidation, that of course, we'd love to hear it. And Susanna read out the following lines:

"Every single morning at 8.30 for years Townes called me for our 'morning call'. Guy would usually bring me a cup of coffee, because he knew we'd be on the phone for at least an hour.

"He'd say, hey babe. Townes was the only man I let call me babe. We talked about art and artists and history, especially Texas history, and Hank Williams and Lightnin' Hopkins and Vincent van Gogh and Indians. We talked about the Bible and European ways and the sky that day and angels and ghosts and demons, and Dylan Thomas and the birds and his dog. We talked about all the different kinds of love, and he'd describe them in detail.

"We talked about the language and words and poetry and songs. More often than not he'd read me his new poem of the day. Songs always had to work as a poem on paper first. Townes' rule.

Townes Van Zandt on stage with Guy, Great American Music Hall, 1992
(Tom Erikson)

"We always agreed about what the first day of spring really was. He'd call and say, hey, this is it, and I would know exactly what he was talking about. I'd say, yep, I was just thinking the same thing. We did that year after year. Sometimes he'd tell me those terrible jokes of his. Sometimes he'd cry, sometimes I'd cry for him. When I told him he drank too much he'd say, hey, there are sober people in India.

"We'd talk about the Andy Griffith Show. He couldn't watch violence on TV, only Nick At Night usually. Yet he'd say, if anyone touches you I'll slit their throat and drink their blood like wine. He'd make me laugh till it hurt regaling me with stories about his wildness. Or he'd let me cry till it didn't hurt. All he'd have to say was, aw babe, and that would work.

"Sometimes I was spellbound – his words were always gentle and loving, but like in his songs, mighty words they were. Sure, sometimes we'd fight about nothing, like the real meaning of the word innocence. Then we'd make jokes out of that word.

"He let me in his soul and I let him in mine. I had the honor and privilege of having this noble wild soul in my life.

"He called me his best friend and god-sister. I called him my best friend and god-brother. We always said I love you before we hung up.

"This morning 8.30 came and the phone didn't ring."

Performance

There is so much respect and admiration for Guy Clark's songwriting that sometimes his performing talent is overlooked. Guy himself has no great opinion of either his voice or his guitar playing, but in fact neither aspect of his performance should be underestimated. His voice has a far greater range than is immediately apparent – if necessary, he can sing a Jimmie Rodgers blue yodel with the best of them – and his guitar playing is simply perfectly suited to the songs he writes. On top of that is his quiet mastery of the stage and his audience. Keith Case remembers the first time he saw Guy play in Nashville:

"I'd been working with him maybe four years or something, he'd been going out with the band primarily – he was based here and I was in Colorado and not travelling a lot right then so I don't think I'd seen him perform for a couple of years at that point – and he hadn't been doing a lot of road work, we'd just been booking very few dates, so when I got to town we cooked up a solo date for him, because at that point the road work was virtually impossible – there just were not dates out there for him that were of a large enough dollar volume to carry a band on these road trips.

"I guess he used to perform solo a lot in Texas, there were a couple of small rooms in Houston he used to play when he lived down there, but I had never seen him that way and I booked him in this terrible place. It was a 'new music' room, for what that meant in 1982 – they played a lot of headbanger music and stuff – this night it turned into a whole different thing. It was just a dark dungeon-like little room, but a very large and good PA and I guess Guy hadn't played in town for a while because the show just sold to the walls. Of course I was there, I couldn't wait to see him, and I was amazed at how moved I was when he walked out and took the stage, this magnetic presence, a dominating, charismatic figure – and that was the first time I heard *The Randall Knife* – I was just extremely moved by his presence, as was the rest of the crowd.

"He keeps complete control over his audience – he's not a showman, in terms of what that usually connotes, and I'd rather hear Guy Clark sing a Guy Clark song than anybody, but in the classic sense he doesn't have a great singing voice, but people love to hear him sing. And he's a really good guitarist. No-one ever talks about it, ever, but he's a fabulous guitar player – maybe that's because the power of the songs so overshadows everything else."

People we interviewed for this book all enthused about Guy's

Guy tuning up on stage, c.1976 (Guy & Susanna Clark collection)

ability as a great storyteller or his conversational songwriting style, but Keith is one of the few who mentioned his guitar playing. Guy himself was quite disparaging when we referred to his playing style, but one of the joys of a song like *Dublin Blues* is the ad lib pacing of the playing: it has a kind of drawing-in effect, almost forcing us to listen and become connected. He plays it as he feels it, and it is this ad lib style that makes each performance a new experience.

Guy tends to play down this aspect: "I can play my songs, you know, pretty much, I can work them all out, but I'm not a guitar player as such, you know, I just don't play guitar very well. I play well on my songs, but if you heard me sit in with somebody, you know, I'm not that kind of guitar player. And I wish I was. Couple of beers and I'll try anything!

"I mean, I know some really good guitar players who just play off the top of your head, they play anything they can think of, you know. I mean, guys who just fuckin' blow you away. My favourites – I like the people I play with. Verlon Thompson, I love his guitar playing, it's just so *right*. And then Darrell Scott is just amazing. I mean, in this town there's a thousand great guitar players, I mean, *great* guitar players. Like I said, what I play for the songs I write, I can play as good as anybody, or better, but..."

Like Archimedes in his bath, Nick had a very strong 'Aha!' moment, sitting with Guy Clark in the den of his home in the hills of Nashville.

"So you play guitar, huh?" Guy drawled.

The strings on his well-worn and well-travelled guitar, custom built by Michael Heider in Vancouver, had been slackened right down for a recent trip. Guy lazily tuned it, handed it to Nick, and threw on the table his home-made thumb pick with plectrum rivetted in the middle.

The moment Nick saw this weird but totally logical tool, it all fell into place for him how Guy achieves the combination of both a clawhammer fingerpicking style and the more conventional country flat pick. It suddenly became clear how this flexibility allows him the freedom to maintain an inherent and very individual rhythm while leaving the spaces that many of his songs demand for their impact; without the use of this pick, the effect would have to be manufactured rather than felt.

In England, the only times we were able to see Guy Clark were the small tours or one-off gigs that took place occasionally, usually in out of the way folk clubs or arts centres around the country:

"Yeah, I've done a lot of them over the years, I don't know how many times. I enjoyed them, sure I did, same as folk clubs anywhere, it's mostly what I play. I still don't enjoy playing real giant places, I don't connect or something."

But touring still seemed to be a fairly haphazard affair. After a strange situation when Guy pulled out of a tour with the veteran cowboy singer Don Edwards at the last moment, the next time we saw him was on a short series of dates Guy and Travis played in small venues, including an arts project in Islington, where both father and son were in top form. Guy's comment is typically low-key ("that was nice, yeah..."), but Travis remembers it particularly fondly: "That Union Chapel gig, that was *it*, it was spectacular!"

There have also been a few memorable television appearances, including *The Session*, made in Ireland in 1989 with Jimmie Dale Gilmore, and *The Transatlantic Sessions*, in Scotland in 1995 (which still hasn't been broadcast in America).

Guy has somewhat mixed feelings about the Scottish experience. As usual, the downside was the way the technical aspects overshadowed the enjoyment of playing with the variety of musicians involved:

"It was fun, but it was kinda tedious because it seemed like they were more interested in the camera angles than the music. I have no idea what it ended up like because I've never seen it, but it was fun doing it. It was several days we stayed at the house, I can't remember exactly how long. May have been a week, I don't know."

Travis also came over for the Transatlantic Sessions, and played bass with some of the other artists as well as Guy. He remembers the time vividly:

"It was very interesting, some of the music, really all the music was pretty amazing. One of the things they did that was strange was, it was all shot on film, so they had five or six cameras, film cameras, and they were shooting all these different shots. So you had to play the song so they could get their focus and figure out what shots they were going to do, and, okay, now play it again! – it was like, you know, *you missed it*, you should have gotten that one!

It was very strange. It wouldn't have been so bad if they had just worried about camera angles, but to try to capture – you know, when you play a song with that group of people you play it once and grab that spontaneity is what I think you should try to do, but they were trying to make us recapture that spontaneity so they could grab it each time. I don't know. But it was a whole lot of fun."

The last two years have seen substantial changes in Guy Clark's career and personal life. The death of Townes Van Zandt in January 1997 hit both him and Susanna particularly hard, and later, in the summer of 1997, Travis decided to give up touring, bringing to a close a successful working partnership that had lasted some five years. Travis explains some of the background behind the decision:

"I needed to stay home! I've got a wife and two kids and a 68-year old house to take care of, and you know, I just can't be out doing it. It's hard on my wife and hard on my kids to not have an extra hand around, and you don't really realise it till you're here and you see what she's doing. Gets pretty crazy around here sometimes.

Guy on stage with Johnny Cash and Waylon Jennings, Harlan Howard birthday bash (Beth Gwinn)

"I haven't played music in quite some time. I'll play for the kids every once in a while, just get out the guitar and play, I don't know, old Rolling Stones songs, whatever comes to my mind and whatever I can croak out of my throat!

"Do I miss it? Ah, some, yeah. I do and I don't. Sometimes I'll be thinking about it and I'll go, boy, that was... I miss Ireland, you know, I miss the Indian food on Frognal! Oh man, I love it! Go to the UK, what do you eat? I'm a vindaloo guy! Yeah, so I miss that kind of stuff, and I miss the people, I miss my dad, I miss the rush of actually playing, you know. I mean, that's a rush, it really is."

Guy seems philosophical about the breakup of the partnership with his son: "Yeah, he's retired! He doesn't play with me any more. It was a good sound. I'm doing some solo stuff now, and sometimes with Darrell Scott, Verlon Thompson, Suzi Ragsdale, the people on the records, just depending on the situation and what the economics of it are. I just refuse to lose money any more!"

Guy Clark still hops around the country and the world, either solo or with friends; and whether it's a festival in California, a convention in Scandinavia or an arts centre in England, still puts his whole being into playing his songs and telling his stories as only he can. And there are rare moments of unexpected public recognition: in July 1998, to promote her OTHER VOICES, TOO album, Nanci Griffith gathered together her Texas friends on David Letterman's nationally broadcast *Late Show* to sing Guy's *Desperados Waiting For a Train*. As on the album version, verses in the song were taken by Rodney Crowell, Jimmie Dale Gilmore, Eric Taylor, Steve Earle, Jerry Jeff Walker, Guy and herself. Guy may have had reservations about the song being performed in that way, but it was still quite something to see all that talent on stage together. Late in 1997, Guy and Susanna also hosted the big tribute concert to Townes Van Zandt that was broadcast on the PBS *Austin City Limits* show.

In recent years Guy Clark has lent his considerable presence to several recording projects by other people. Apart from Ramblin' Jack Elliott's FRIENDS OF MINE and Nanci Griffith's OTHER VOICES albums previously mentioned, Guy sings and Travis plays bass on Kate Campbell's 1997 MOONPIE DREAMS. Kate is one of the brighter young talents in the folk/country field, bringing in elements of jazz and blues to her recordings. *Bud's Sea-Mint Boat* is a charming, gentle story, very Clarkian in character and an ideal vehicle for Guy's vocals – he takes a verse and sings harmonies through the song.

Guy's popularity in Norway, bolstered by his appearances at the 'Down On the Farm' festival there, introduced him to a local duo, Somebody's Darling; the singer, Tine Valand, went solo and moved to Austin, Texas in the mid nineties, where she recorded an album at Cedar Creek Studio. As well as her version of *She Ain't Goin' Nowhere*, the album contains a duet with Guy on Tom Russell's waltz-time *Mineral Wells*.

He also sings on the most recent Chip Taylor CD. Taylor is the writer of such seminal pop songs from the sixties as *Wild Thing* and *Angel of the Morning* and country classics like *The Real Thing* and *Early Sunday Morning*, but gave up the music business for the racetrack, gambling professionally for some twenty years. Since his return to music, he has recorded two albums and started touring again. The second album, SEVEN DAYS IN MAY, has a duet with Guy Clark (on the appropriately titled *One Hell of a Guy*) and a nice note on the sleeve: 'Guy, you were one of the first ones to welcome me back and invite me on stage when I traded the horses for my guitar – thanks so much for that – but did you have to sing so damn good on our duet?!'

I Don't Love You Much Do I

Our conversations with Guy Clark's friends and colleagues produced much material that was not just biographical or related to Guy's work, but was more personal in nature. The difficulty was where in the book to place it, the context of most of this material not relating to anything specific in Guy's life or career. Finally we decided simply to devote a chapter to these tributes to Guy Clark, as a friend, from people who are able to put into words what so many of his admirers all over the world would like to say. The remarks are in no particular order, except that we start off with one of his oldest friends, Gary B. White, since we couldn't – and didn't want to – stop him talking!

Gary B. White: "In this business there's a handful of guys that just maintain their human aspects and are not tainted by show business and basically they stay down to earth, and the two that always come to mind are Guy and Kris Kristofferson. I mean, if Guy comes to town he always calls and says, I'm playing over at McCabe's, or the Crazy Horse, come down; he always asks me to get up on stage and perform a couple of songs. He's not a person who's seeking fame, I think he just wanted to be the best craftsman he could possibly be, and I think that's what he's achieved; he did it.

"The first guitar he built was beautiful, you know, that's the way he pursues things. But not for the fame, not to lord it over people or be above anybody, that was not his issue. It was, gee if I do this I can make a living and be my own boss and be in charge of everything, the production and quality of it, then nobody can come along and say, yeah, but we wanted you to write about this or that. So I just see him as a guy who took charge of his life, who was independent and didn't want other people writing it for him; and if he couldn't have started a tune he would probably have been the world's foremost cabinet maker or something. He's just of that quality and perseverance.

"He helped me build a banjo neck, you know. I said, I can't do that, and he said, oh yeah, you just take some wood and start working it. I'll help you pick out a piece, we'll go over and get some maple wood. So we sent off to this company that does ebony fingerboards

Texas–1992 (Peter Figen)

and we built this whole neck for this old banjo I had, and it's a piece of art, it's all inlaid with mother of pearl and carved. I have never before or since done anything like that, but with Guy he just said, oh you can do it, you just get down and do it, here I'll show you how. And anything he took on, whether it was the first time or not, he did it with alacrity. And so, I wasn't surprised that Guy Clark would be a great songwriter, not at all.

"Jerry Jeff generally calls when he comes into town, he has more of an entourage, his schedule gets real hectic. Guy just comes out, gets off the plane with a suitcase and a guitar and ambles over to wherever he's working, gives me a call and we meet up and generally have dinner. Every time I've seen him, I'd say in the last twelve years it's been out here on my turf because I just haven't had the reason to get to Nashville, which is unfortunate, but it's hard to maintain a 3000 mile relationship!

"I got a very nice telephone call from him recently, I don't recall what it was, probably over the last Christmas holiday, and he said, I was just twirling the Rolodex and calling people and wanted to talk to you, and I said, that's it, you're not coming out or anything? and he said, no, I just missed the sound of your voice, wanted to say hi. So he's a very constant and sincere and forthright person, and he cares about his friends, and at that time he said, do you have Keith Sykes' number in Memphis? I said, yeah, I just talked to Keith, how about Carl Snyder? He gave me a number and said call Carl, he'd love to hear from you, and so I did. But Guy would precipitate that kind of thing, you know, sometimes I'd get a call saying hey, I'm at this party, bumped into an old friend of yours, Paul Geremiah, and I said, where are you – New York! what, you just called up? – yeah, he said, I knew he'd like to talk to you so I just put it on my telephone bill. I don't want to say we haven't been close lately, because I'll always feel close to Guy, but whether we're miles apart or years apart, he always maintains that contact.

"One other little thing of note too that he has also travelled for a while with Townes Van Zandt, and they'd come out together. Just before Townes died they came out and Guy would get a job, I think he was really just trying to help Townes out because Guy takes care of business when Townes really couldn't, he had a lot of skeletons in his closet and sort of a determination to have life go bad around him

– typical of blues and country singers! – but I know Townes was also part of the Sand Mountain Coffee House and the Jesters Cabaret crowd, and when Guy came out here to work he would generally ask them, you know, as long as I'm coming can my buddy Townes be the opening act – oh, wow, Townes Van Zandt, he's great – so Townes would come out and I'd get to see both of them a lot and it was always a pleasure."

TOWNES VAN ZANDT (from the Richard Wootton interview): "Everybody in Nashville loves Guy Clark. It's the way he is, he's so sincere 'n' all and so straight ahead. The people in Nashville are real suspective… they're rednecks – real nice rednecks – but rednecks most of them. Put a whole lot of value on 100% sincerity and manners, courtesy to ladies, all that, and Guy's naturally that way. I've never met anybody that didn't like him."

RODNEY CROWELL: "My relationship with Guy as a friend – I love him and I'm a friend for life, a loyal friend, whatever he needs from me I'll be there with it. I think that as a younger man my relationship with Guy was so much born out of awe and respect, and basically I emulated Guy for years, you know, because I just loved his integrity, his demeanor, just the gravity of his intelligence and his commitment as an artist. Over the years as I've grown, you know, matured and become a full man, it's turned into, I love Guy and respect him as an artist and as a man."

DARRELL SCOTT: "Yeah, I think he's a wonderful man, he's a gentleman, he's fair and sensitive to other people, he's very much somebody I admire. I think he's someone who's been, you know, there and back, whatever there is, whether it's hell or emotions or good times or bad times, yeah, he's a great man, great.

"And the pleasure of playing with Guy, that's the trip for me, to respond to some of the best writing we've got. Like working on the live album and doing *That Old Time Feelin'*, I mean how does it get better than that as a player, someone who's a writer too, to respond to songs like that with a mandolin or a guitar in your hands? Man, that's as good as it gets, it really is."

Keith Case: "There's so many facets, you know, he's the best good ol' boy you ever saw; if you want to go out and howl at night, ah, he's kinda given it up now because he knows I resist, but he used to come by and try to drag me out to the bars at lunchtime and stuff, because Guy's a partyer extraordinaire. But he's a classic gentleman, and a classic ladies' man, I just admire him in so many different ways, and he's one of my dearest friends, just a fabulous guy. And I guess the respect you see here in the Nashville community – there isn't a big star in this town that when asked to talk about songwriting doesn't bring up Guy Clark. He's just a wonderful individual, he's kind and giving, and fair – fair as anybody on the planet. I value my relationship with him enormously."

Nanci Griffith: "He's just consistently a brilliant writer, you know, he continues to write great songs that are immediately memorable, and follow along the lines of folk songwriting. Like Pete Seeger has always said, his job is to put song on to the lips of babes, as opposed to being a star, and so those are the qualities that I find in Guy's writing, that will make him a lifelong endearment to me. Guy's just this great role model and he's a wonderful pal and a great friend."

Emmylou Harris: "He has tremendous insight, and it comes from who he is and the way he looks at life, from his point of view, it's unique. And a point of view is so important in writers, it's not just a matter of making things rhyme and being clever, there has to be something else going on there that stands the test of time. He's a true poet – for me he's fast becoming the poet laureate of songwriters.

"And he's a great *American* writer. There is something about this country, about our philosophy, something that makes us unique as a people, considering that we are a hodgepodge of everything – we definitely do have an identity, and every once in a while someone, like Walt Whitman, comes along and really picks up on that, especially in that talent of being able to spin a yarn, and tell a story. Guy's quite a storyteller, and I've always been a sucker for a story song. It's almost like reading a short story, the characters are so beautifully drawn.

"And he's so funny, so bright. Just a conversation with him is like a great song! One of the reasons I wanted to move to Nashville was to be around people that I felt emotionally attached to as well as creatively. And the friendship has endured."

JERRY JEFF WALKER: "Guy's a better person than I am, and he'll be the first to admit it! He's a great gentleman, a true craftsman, and he loves the art of songwriting – he puts it on a higher level, and I think he makes everybody try a little harder. Because we know he's doing it that way. I once saw a song – Guy was working on a sheet of paper and there was like a word crossed out and I looked at it and said, is this like the third draft, and he said, no, this is the original one. He was writing the whole song and he's only crossed out one word! The song was *Coat From the Cold*, and I've been thinking about that ever since."

HOLGER PETERSEN: "It's the imagery in Guy's songs, the detail, the soulfulness, the storytelling craft of it. I always think of Guy and Townes together as songwriters, and the two of them setting a certain standard that people aspire to. And no matter how many times I see him, and how often I hear those songs whether it's on record or live, so many times I'm just struck by a new line or phrase or word or whatever, and it's like hearing it for the first time.

"There's so much depth in his craft and his ability, you know, I never tire of hearing Guy perform those songs live because every time I listen there's always a new experience to be had. It's his straightahead delivery, and the quiet way, the elegant way – he doesn't hammer anybody over the head, he just draws them in. He does have that charisma on stage and he does have that sly sense of humour, you know, that shows up in so many songs. And it can take you to Texas, it can take you to Ireland, it can take you anywhere.

"And one thing that always stays with me is his phrase, 'When in Rome, burn Roman candles!' One he's pulled out at the odd party and one I use all the time now!"

JIM MCGUIRE: "I look at Guy almost as a brother in a way, we're both the same age; we both sort of started our careers here at the same time and both developed as artists at the same time. I don't know what to say except he's just been a great friend for many years and I think of him as a brother."

TRAVIS CLARK: "He's it, he's pretty much the beans! His contemporaries pay him as much or more kudos than the fan base, he's amazing."

MILES WILKINSON: "Guy's the best, you know."

POSTSCRIPT

It is the evening of Monday 21 September 1998. In the great ballroom of the Opryland Hotel in Nashville, the American Society of Composers, Authors and Publishers is holding its 36th annual country music awards banquet. The vice-president of ASCAP, Connie Bradley, hosts the black-tie gala evening, and a thousand of Nashville's great and good sit down to applaud their peers: songwriters and publishers of the most performed and most acclaimed country songs of the year. Even some of Tennessee's politicians are honoured for their support in the legislature of country music and the rights of its creators. And in the midst of this, one very special presentation is made.

Lyle Lovett comes to the rostrum holding an award in the shape of an unprepossessing clear pyramid set on a base with a simple inscription engraved on the front. He says a few well chosen words before asking the recipient to come forward and accept the award, its significance clearly defined by the words inscribed on it: "The ASCAP Foundation Lifetime Achievement Award, presented to Guy Clark for his outstanding accomplishments as a songwriter, recording artist and musical mentor in the field of country music."

The reaction of the audience is overwhelming – Guy's response is simply "Breathtaking!" To those closest to Guy it seems that the younger members of the audience are thinking, this is what it's all about, while the older ones are saying, this reminds us of what we're doing here in the first place. Connie Bradley later tells Rodney Crowell that it is the most beautiful moment in all her years at ASCAP.

Rodney comes on with Vince Gill and performs a couple of Guy's songs as a brief musical tribute; Guy pays tribute himself to his wife and to the friends who provided encouragement and support during the 27 years since he and Susanna first moved to Nashville, and says, "I figure that if I stay for ten more years I'll probably break even!"

Which shows what really matters to those who really matter. "Whatever we're in this for," says Susanna, "it's not business!" She finds it hard to explain in mere words just how much the fact of Guy being so honoured means to her, but tells how she and Guy were inspired to start writing a song together as soon as they got back home from the banquet.

So what of the future? "I don't really make any long term career plans," says Guy, "just keep playing till the money runs out! To me it's successful if I write 10, 12 songs for a new album, that's as far as

At the workbench, Nashville, 1998 (Jeff Horne)

I get. I've got one so far! That's what I'm planning on."

Several of Guy Clark's friends, Miles Wilkinson in particular, have mentioned to us how importantly they regard his current involvement with building classical guitars; there is an element, they feel, of bringing him full circle back to the time he first started playing guitar himself, to the Mexican music of his early mentor, Lola Bonner, and to his eventual – and, it seems, inevitable – discovery of the craft of songbuilding.

Even if Guy Clark were never to write another song in his life, his work would stand as a legacy to be drawn upon for inspiration and example as long as there are poets and craftsmen left in the world. But there are more great songs waiting to be written: he will write them, he will play them, and those of us who recognise the honesty and integrity in the writing will, as they have done throughout his career, pick them up and pass them on.

In the meantime, what about this idea of a second live album using the unreleased rehearsed material from KEEPERS?

"I may do it, but not soon. Hopefully I'll be able to write some more songs! And I fought them tooth and nail not to put those two new ones on there, but they said no, no, if you're going to do a live album you're going to have to put some new stuff on it. Well, okay… so now I can't do them on a new album! So now that's two more I gotta write. Ah, I just compromise at every turn – I'm just fuckin' putty in their hands! So *no more Mr Nice Guy!* Hmm, I have to write that down…"

INDEX